Fission Girl

Melanie Fine

July 16, 1945 5:29:45 a.m. Trinity site, Alamogordo, New Mexico

And there was the sense of this ominous cloud hanging over us. It was so brilliant purple with all the radioactive glowing and it just seemed to hang there forever. Of course it didn't. It must have been a very short time until it went up. It was very terrifying and the thunder from the blast, it bounced on the rocks and then it went — I don't know where else it bounced but it never seemed to stop – not like an ordinary echo with thunder. It just kept echoing back and forth. It was a very scary time when it went off and I wish I would remember what my brother said but I can't. But I think we just said, 'It worked.' I think that's what we both said, both of us. "It worked."

- Frank Oppenheimer, brother of Robert Oppenheimer, the Manhattan Project.

1901, Vienna, Austria

Lise Meitner, born Elise Meitner, began her physics studies at the University of Vienna in 1901. She was one of the first women to be admitted to the University, for which she had to prepare privately, as Vienna's version of high school at the time was only open to men.

Lise was born to secular Jewish parents in 1878. Her great-grandfather had come from the village of Meietheiner in Moravia. On Friday nights in Moravia, he would sneak around the village, laying a loaf of challah at the doorsteps of Jews who could not afford their own.

Lise studied physics under Anton Lampa, Stefan Meyer and Ludwig Boltzmann. The latter was well-known for his passionate clinging to the theory of atoms as the basic building block of matter. His view of the existence of atoms invited as many critics as supporters, compelling him to spend much of his time defending his beliefs with colleagues. Lise was enamored by Boltzmann and, according to her nephew Otto Robert Frisch, "Boltzmann gave her the vision of physics as a battle for ultimate truth, a vision she never lost."

In 1900, the year before Lise's matriculation, English physicist Lord Kelvin addressed a group of physicists at the British Association for the Advancement of Science in 1900 saying, "There is nothing new to be discovered in physics now. All that remains is more and more precise measurement."

While Kelvin was addressing this assemblage of English physicists, German physicist Max Planck presented his theory that light could only be given off in discrete units known as quanta. These quanta, the discrete packets of energy, became known as photons. As a result, light could be seen as both an electromagnetic wave of energy, and a particle. These "tiny" packets known as quanta gave birth to quantum physics, which would come to revolutionize the physics community and the world.

Meitner begin her physics studies at the precipice of this new physics.

December 10, 1903 Stockholm, Sweden

Henri Becquerel, Marie and Pierre Curie received the 1903 Nobel Prize in Physics "in recognition of the extraordinary services [Becquerel] has rendered by his discovery of spontaneous radioactivity," and jointly to Pierre Curie and Marie Curie, née Sklodowska "in recognition of the extraordinary services they have rendered by their joint researches on the radiation phenomena discovered by Professor Henri Becquerel." The Curies were too ill to attend the ceremony in person. At the time, no one, not even the Curies, knew the effects of long-term exposure to radiation. Rather, they, along with the larger scientific community, were enamored with the discovery of radioactivity, so much so, that Marie would keep the bluish-green glowing radium by her bedside.

Pierre attend the Stockholm ceremony the following year on his and Marie's behalf.

In Vienna at that time, girls' education finished at 14 years old. Girls were not accepted at the University of Vienna until the year 1897. Lise immediately wanted to enroll. However, since girls were not allowed to attend the Viennese equivalent of high school, Lise had to study privately to pass the *Matura*, the series of exams given at the completion of secondary school.

In 1896, while 18-year-old Lise was preparing for this exam, Henri Becquerel in France made some interesting observations in his lab. Becquerel wrote his doctoral thesis on phosphorescence, how materials glow-in-the-dark after they have been exposed to light.

X-rays had only been recently discovered by William Conrad Roentgen at the time. Becquerel thought that perhaps the phosphorescent light that uranium salts emitted after being exposed to sunlight were the very same X-rays Roentgen discovered. He placed the uranium salts outside on top of a photographic plate that was covered in thick black paper to protect the plate itself from getting exposed to sunlight. If the image of the salts appeared on the photographic plate once it was developed, it would mean that the salts emitted their own X-rays onto the photographic plate.

Serendipitously, during a few overcast days in Paris, Becquerel left his uranium salt and photographic plate apparatus in his desk drawer. He decided to develop the plate anyway, even though it hadn't been exposed to sunlight, expecting to find a very weak image. "Instead," wrote Becquerel, "the silhouettes appeared with great intensity."

Becquerel tried the same experiment on non-phosphorescent uranium salts, a form of uranium that didn't seem to give off light at all, and got the same results, placing them on photographic plates without exposing them to sunlight. Apparently, these uranium salts gave off their own penetrating radiation that came from within!

Marie and Pierre Curie dubbed this radiation radioactivity, and they were fascinated by it. Marie wondered whether elements other than uranium were similarly radioactive. She tested a number of items borrowed from the Natural History Museum of France, ultimately discovering that both thorium and pitchblende were radioactive.

Pitchblende is the black amorphous source of uranium ore, containing up to 80% uranium. When Marie and Pierre successively isolated the uranium from the pitchblende, they were surprised to find that the remaining pitchblende was four times as radioactive as the uranium itself.

The two of them spent the next year isolating the source of radioactivity from the pitchblende. With each chemical process, they'd keep the radioactive part and dispose of the rest. With each subsequent process, their sample of radioactive material got smaller and smaller until only the pure radioactive material was left.

Marie asked a colleague to identify the specimen using a spectrograph. A spectrograph of an element is akin to an element's fingerprint. Each element of the Periodic Table emits a distinct spectrum of colors similar to the rainbow. Since Marie's radioactive material did not emit the same spectrum as any known element, she knew she had a new element on her hands, and named it Polonium, in honor of her Polish birthplace.

Marie and Pierre would spend the next year isolating a pure form of another new radioactive element, radium, which was one million times more radioactive than uranium.

1905 Bern, Switzerland

Albert Einstein, while serving as a patent clerk in Switzerland, published an unprecedented four papers in 1905, including his dissertation. These four papers were on:

The Photoelectric Effect (which gave rise to quantum theory)
Brownian Motion (provided evidence to support atomic theory)
Special Relativity
$E=mc^2$

In Einstein's paper on $E=mc^2$, Einstein theorized mass was related to energy, and, in cases in which mass is completely converted to energy, determines the amount of energy created.

April 19, 1906 Paris, France

Pierre Curie was killed when he was hit and subsequently run over by a horse and carriage.

September 5, 1906 Duino, Italy

While on summer vacation in Duino, a seaside resort on the northern Adriatic coast in Northeastern Italy, Ludwig Boltzmann, Lise Meitner's teacher and mentor and a lifelong sufferer of bipolar disorder, hanged himself.

Lise Meitner received her doctorate in physics that same year, becoming the second woman in history to earn a physics doctorate from the University of Vienna.

She also met Max Planck, the father of quantum theory, when he traveled to Vienna to pay his respects to the late Boltzmann.

Early 1907 Berlin, Germany

After trying her hand at teaching, Lise moved to Berlin to see if she could find work as a physicist. She asked Max Planck if she could sit in on his lectures at the University of Berlin. Though Planck questioned why someone with a doctorate in physics would need his lectures, he acquiesced. Over time, Planck became her mentor and close friend. She was a frequent guest at the Planck home, where Planck would often serenade his guests on the piano.

At the University of Berlin Lise met her lifetime professional collaborator Otto Hahn.

Otto Hahn was known as a radiochemist, a chemist conducting research in the burgeoning field of radioactivity. In 1907, preparing the radioactive samples was the work of chemists, and interpreting the radioactive pathways was the work of physicists. As such, Meitner and Hahn formed a collaboration that would complement each other's strengths and weaknesses.

Bringing Lise into the chemistry department of the University of Berlin was no small task. Emile Fischer, the chairman of the Chemistry Institute, refused to let women into the lab for fear that their hair would catch fire. Apparently, Fischer had once had a Russian student with an "exotic" hair style. As women weren't legally admitted to Prussian universities anyway, Fischer was seemingly generous when he let Meitner work in a former carpenter's shop in the university's basement, acceptable for its separate outside entrance. To use the bathroom, Lise had to patronage a restaurant down the street.

July 17, 1908 Manchester, England

The English physicist Ernest Rutherford, along with his assistants Hans Geiger and Ernest Marsden, published a paper on their experiments with the scattering of alpha particles by matter. This Geiger-Marsden experiment is often referred to as the Gold Foil experiment. They aimed alpha particles, a product of the radiation of radium, at thin gold foil, only a few atoms thick. They had expected the particles to go right through the foil, but a few of them were deflected by the foil and some bounced straight back.

He credited Lise Meitner's previous work in the scattering of alpha particles as an impetus for this study. Though well known in scientific circles, Lise was not an employee of the University of Berlin, as there was almost no path by which a woman could assume a university position.

September 29, 1908 Germany

Lise Meitner converted from Judaism to Protestantism.

October 13, 1908 Karlsruhe, Germany

Fritz Haber, a German Jewish chemist, filed his patent for the "synthesis of ammonia from its elements." As early as 1898 it had been predicted that the world's population was growing at a faster rate than farms could support. The problem was that, in order to increase produce yields, farms needed more nitrogen than the soil provided naturally. It's not that there wasn't enough nitrogen in the world. That was hardly the case. The air is 78% nitrogen. It's just that the nitrogen in the air was not in a form that is absorbable by plants.

Plants need nitrogen for a number of things, most importantly, as a component of both chlorophyll, which turns sun energy into sugar, and amino acids, the building blocks of proteins.

Nitrogen gas, when reacted with hydrogen gas, produces ammonia, NH_3, which is water soluble, according to the following chemical equation:

$$N_2(g) + 3H_2(g) \rightarrow 2NH_3(g)$$

Being water soluble, ammonia can be absorbed into the soil, whereby it changes to saltpeter nitrogen, a form useful to plants.

Haber developed his method for "nitrogen fixation," the process whereby nitrogen from the atmosphere can be changed to a form that can be absorbed by crops by combining together nitrogen and hydrogen with a catalyst under high pressure conditions.

December 10, 1908 Stockholm, Sweden

Ernest Rutherford accepted the 1908 Nobel Prize in Chemistry in Stockholm, Sweden for his discovery of the disintegration of elements into different elements, known as transmutation. Like his contemporaries Becquerel and the Curies, Rutherford had focused his research on the radioactivity of various substances, which gave off gaseous emanations and became altogether new elements.

This was a great challenge to then-modern turn-of-the-century scientists. By the end of the nineteenth century, scientists had come together and agreed on the existence of the atom as the smallest building block of matter. According to John Dalton's Atomic Theory circa 1805, atoms were the basic units of matter. Atoms could be rearranged to form new compounds, but they could not be created nor destroyed.

When Rutherford was studying the radioactive element thorium, he noticed that thorium gave off a gaseous substance called a thorium emanation. This emanation came only from an intermediate product of thorium named thorium-X. Thorium-X is continually and spontaneously produced from thorium, which further decays into this gaseous emanation, which can be condensed into a liquid, and precipitates as a solid when it touches objects in its path. This same emanation is given off by other radioactive elements such as uranium and polonium.

Rutherford further identified that, when radioactive elements disintegrated, they gave off one of two forms of radiation, alpha particles and beta particles.

The fact that atoms themselves can spontaneously be transmuted into other atoms was the holy grail of the alchemists of old, the progenitors of scientific practice, who tasked themselves with finding cures for diseases, the elixir of youth, and turning base metals into gold, among others.

Rutherford visited the lab of Lise Meitner and Otto Hahn shortly after winning the Nobel Prize. After learning that Meitner was a woman — for some reason he hadn't known that, as scientific publications authored by her read "L. Meitner" -- she was made to accompany Rutherford's wife Christmas shopping while Hahn and Rutherford talked science.

1911 Ludwigshafen-Oppau, Germany

The first ammonia plant was established at Ludwigshafen-Oppau, Germany, using Haber's process of nitrogen fixing. By 1913, this plant was producing over 30 tons of fixed nitrogen per day.

April 1911 Manchester, England

Ernest Rutherford published the paper "The Scattering of Alpha and Beta Particles by Matter and the Structure of the Atom" which proposed a new model of the atom as having a dense, positive center called the nucleus, based on his experimental work shooting alpha particles at gold foil.

In a 1938 address given at Cambridge University, Rutherford recalled his findings:

> It was quite the most incredible event that has ever happened to me in my life. It was almost as incredible as if you fired a 15-inch shell at a piece of tissue paper and it came back and hit you. On consideration, I realized that this scattering backward must be the result of a single collision, and when I made calculations I saw that it was impossible to get anything of that order of magnitude unless you took a system in which the greater part of the mass of the atom was concentrated in a minute nucleus. It was then that I had the idea of an atom with a minute massive centre, carrying a charge.

Atoms, according to Rutherford's atomic model, were the building blocks of matter, and within each atom existed a small, dense positive nucleus, surrounded by negatively charged electrons. Inside that positive nucleus existed positively charged particles called protons.

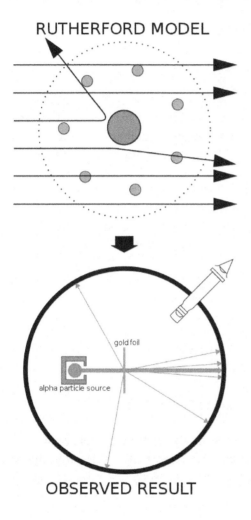

RUTHERFORD MODEL

OBSERVED RESULT

The nucleus itself was impenetrable... or so they thought.

Summer 1911 Dahlem-Berlin, Germany

Construction began on the new Kaiser Wilhelm Institute for Chemistry in Dahlem, a southwestern part of Berlin. Because of the rapid growth of scientific research, a new form of funded German research emerged, financed privately without university or state interference. The Kaiser Wilhelm Institute was that place. Not just the institute for chemistry, but as many as 30 Kaiser Wilhelm Institutes broke ground around the same time, or even later, such as the:

Kaiser Wilhelm Institute (KWI) for Biology

KWI for Biophysics

KWI for Physics, of which Albert Einstein was the director from 1917 to an auspicious day in 1933.

Because these institutes were independent of academic institutions, many of them came with no teaching obligations whatsoever, so that the scientists could devote one hundred percent of their time to research. Otto Hahn took a position in the KWI for Chemistry as a scientific associate, with the title Professor. Lise Meitner, his research partner in all his chemical endeavors, as well as having her own significant reputation as a physicist, was not offered remuneration because of her gender, but was given the option to join Hahn as a guest.

1912 Berlin, Germany

Late in 1912, Max Planck hired Lise as his Assistant (official title). Though she had been the author of numerous scientific journal articles, this was her first paid position as a physicist.

June 1913 Manchester, England to Berlin, Germany

James Chadwick was graduated from the Victoria University of Manchester with a masters degree in science under Ernest Rutherford. Upon graduation, he took a fellowship to study under Hans Geiger in Berlin.

July 3, 1913

Albert Einstein was elected a member of the Prussian Academy of Sciences in Berlin. The following week, Max Planck visited him, along with Walter Nernst, to convince him to move to Berlin. Planck offered him the directorship of the Kaiser Wilhelm Institute for Physics.

That same month, Danish physicist Niels Bohr collaborated with Ernest Rutherford to publish a paper on the orbital theory of an atom's electrons.

Since Ernest Rutherford had published his model of the atom in 1911, many scientists of the time believed that an atom's electrons orbited around the nucleus, held in orbit by the electrical attraction between the positive charge of the nucleus and negative charge of the electron, much like the planets orbit around the sun because of their gravitational attraction.

The question of the day was, why wouldn't the electrons eventually lose energy and fall into the nucleus? When electrons, even electrons moving at constant speed, continually change directions — which is what they do when they move in a circle — they are accelerating. The definition of acceleration is a change in velocity, either in speed or direction. When an electrical charge accelerates, it gives off electromagnetic radiation, what we know as light. This light, or electromagnetic radiation, comes from the kinetic energy, or speed, of the electrons. This loss of kinetic energy happens almost instantly. And this loss of energy would be given off as a continual spectrum of light, much like raindrops diffract sunlight into a rainbow.

According to Niels Bohr's new paper, electrons circle the nucleus in quantized orbits; that is, orbits of certain energy. What this means is that electrons couldn't be any distance from the nucleus, but only in fixed distances, or orbits.

Bohr deduced this by looking at the light given off by electrifying atoms of certain elements. We see this all the time in the form of neon lights. Neon lights are made of sealed tubes of neon gas. When neon is electrified, it gives off red light. The truth is, many so-called neon lights contain additional gases besides neon to glow in colors other than red. For example, helium gives off orange light, argon gives off lavender, krypton gives off gray or green, mercury vapor gives off light blue, and xenon gives off gray or blue.

Returning to neon, if you looked more closely at the red light from neon through a diffraction grating, you would see that neon's red light is actually a mixture of a consistent number of colored lines:

The fact that these lines are distinct and not a continual rainbow —
like the rainbow you see after rain when the sun reflects off water
droplets — told scientists that only certain energy orbits are allowed
for neon. In other words, when electrons jumped from a higher orbit
further away from the nucleus to an orbit closer to the nucleus, a
certain amount of energy is given off. The energy that is given off in
the visible light spectrum in neon forms the colors above.

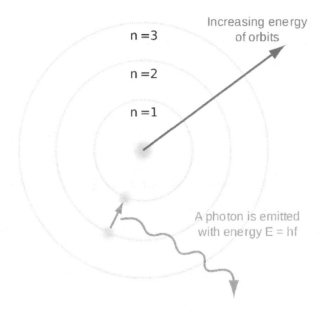

The center of this image is the nucleus. Electrons travel in circular orbits around the nucleus, designated above as n = 1, n = 2 and n = 3. When electrons absorb energy, they jump to higher energy orbits further away from the atom's nucleus. When electrons relax and move back to lower energy orbits, they release that energy in the form of light, indicated above as "a photon is emitted with energy E = hf." The colored spectral lines in helium's spectrograph above each represent one distinct jump from a higher orbit to a lower one.

Bohr's theory of quantized orbits built on Max Planck's theory of quantum mechanics which the latter had introduced at the turn of the century. Max Planck had shown that light existed in discrete packets of energy known as photons, and Albert Einstein had built on this theory in his paper on the photoelectric effect, for which he was awarded the 1921 Nobel Prize in physics.

April 1, 1914 Berlin, Germany

Albert Einstein and his wife moved to Berlin to join the Academy. After a few months, his wife Maric returned with the children to Zurich, after learning that one of Einstein's reasons for moving to Berlin was an ongoing romantic relationship between him and his first cousin Elsa.

Einstein joined Max Planck's social circle that included Lise Meitner, and he often accompanied Planck on the piano with his violin.

June 28, 1914 Sarajevo

Archduke Franz Ferdinand of Austria was assassinated by Serbian Gavrilo Princip in Sarajevo, triggering a chain of events that resulted in the outbreak of World War I.

The construction of the Kaiser Wilhelm Institute for Physics, of which Einstein was to be the director, was delayed with war on the horizon.

July 28, 1914 World War I

One month after the assassination of Archduke Franz Ferdinand, World War I officially began.

Fritz Haber devoted the resources of his Kaiser Wilhelm Institute to the war effort. He combined his work in ammonia synthesis with Wilhelm Ostwald's process for oxidizing ammonia to nitric acid to turn Germany into a self-reliant source of wartime explosives.

German intellectuals, including many prominent scientists, took up the banner of German nationalism, convincing themselves that they were in the "right" and that this war would end soon, Germany being victorious.

Albert Einstein, on the other hand, was one of only four intellectuals who signed a letter condemning the war called a "Manifesto to Europeans," which challenged militarism, referred to the war as "this barbarous war" and called for "educated people in all countries [to] use their influence to bring about a peace treaty that will not carry the seeds of future wars."

James Chadwick, being an Englishman in Berlin, was taken captive as a prisoner of war and interred at the Ruhleben internment camp.

April 22, 1915 Ypres, Belgium

Responding to military requests for tear gas and other irritants, Haber devoted his chemical expertise to experiment with chlorine gas. On this day, during the Second Battle of Ypres, Belgium, French and Algerian soldiers noticed a yellow-gray-colored cloud floating in their direction. As the gas descended over them, they found it hard to breathe, gasping for air and frothing at the mouth. They ran away, leaving behind their rifles. Afraid of the effects of these gases on themselves, the German troops failed to take advantage of the retreat.

400 tons of chlorine gas were used, resulting in the deaths of 6000 Allied soldiers. Fritz Haber was on hand in Ypres that morning to see the effects of his work.

During the war, Lise Meitner served as an X-ray technician on the Austrian front, while Otto Hahn worked alongside Haber in the German gas warfare unit.

Meanwhile, on the opposite side of the war in France, Marie Curie, founding director of France's Red Cross Radiology Service, along with her daughter Irene Joliot-Curie, fundraised for mobile X-ray units which they operated on the front lines, as well as setting up a training program at the Radium Institute to teach other women to operate the equipment.

May 2, 1915 Berlin, Germany

Fritz Haber's wife Clara Immerwahr, herself a chemist, had been mortified by her husband's role in the war, and his perversion of science into a killing machine.

After her party guests had gone home for the evening, Clara walked out to the garden and shot herself in the heart with her husband's service revolver. She was discovered by her son Hermann, who held her in his arms as she died the following morning.

November 11, 1915 Stockholm, Sweden

The Nobel committee announced that Max von Laue had been awarded the 1914 Nobel Prize in Physics for his discovery that X-rays could be diffracted by crystals, revealing two significant finds — one, that X-rays were indeed a form of light waves and not particles, as the latter had been suggested, and two, that the molecular structures of crystals could be teased out by studying how the crystals diffracted X-ray light.

We are able to see things because waves of visible light bounce off a subject and reflect back toward our eyes. Visible light, however, is only a small fraction of all forms of light, between wavelengths of 380 nanometers to 700 nanometers, known as the electromagnetic spectrum. To understand the smallness of these wavelengths, know that a sheet of paper is approximately 100,000 nanometers thick.   700 nanometers are approximately 1/140th smaller than that sheet of paper. Still 380 nm to 700 nm is too large to see an atom. A gold atom, for instance, is approximately a third of a nanometer in diameter. The wavelength of visible light could not bounce off the gold atom and reflect back to our eyes because it simply is too large to "see" the atom in its wake. Only a wavelength smaller than a third of a nanometer could do that, making X-rays, with wavelengths between 0.01 to 10 nanometers, the best choice at the time.

1916

Haber was appointed the chief of Germany's Chemical Warfare Service.

1917 Berlin, Germany

While Otto continued to work for the German war effort, Lise, having finished her war service, returned to their laboratory. She worked diligently there to find the element that transmuted, by giving off an alpha particle, to actinium.

The only evidence that this mother element — or so it's called because it decays into the daughter element, in this case actinium — existed is that in their silica residue from uranium ore, the amount of actinium was increasing. The only way it could be increasing was if more of it was being made. In traditional chemistry, elements are not "made," other than in star furnaces in the galaxies. Rather, elements are immutable, and can only be rearranged in chemical reactions. However, this new science of radioactivity showed that elements can actually be "made" into other elements. Using what Lise learned in studying radioactivity decay sequences, she predicted the existence of an element that decayed into actinium, and eventually she and Hahn were able to isolate and identify it.

They named the new element protactinium, the precursor of actinium, for which she was awarded the Leibniz Medal of the Berlin Academy of Sciences.   That same year she was granted her own physics section at the Kaiser Wilhelm Institute for Chemistry.

March 16, 1918 Berlin, Germany

Lise Meitner and Otto Hahn published their paper, "The Mother Substance of Actinium, a New Radioactive Element of Long Half-life." Though Lise had done most of the work while Hahn was performing his war service, Hahn's name was listed first on the paper due to Lise's deep loyalty to their partnership. Would that loyalty be reciprocated twenty years later, we would soon find out.

June 23, 1918 Berlin, Germany

Lise wrote in a letter to Otto Hahn:

> Did I write to you that I recently gave[i] a colloquium on our work, and that Planck, Einstein, and Rubens told me afterwards how good it was? From which you can see that I gave quite a decent lecture, even though I was, stupidly enough, again very self-conscious…. I was glad you weren't there, you would surely have scolded me. This way, I quickly got over my shyness with a friendly jest from Planck and a very comforting psychological observation from Einstein…. I am optimistic enough to expect peace by autumn so I hope that we can again work together next winter."

November 11, 1918 5:00 am Compiégne, France

Germany signed an armistice agreement with the Allies in a railroad car outside Compiégne, France, ending World War I.

After the war, Fritz Haber became the director of the Kaiser Wilhelm Institute in Chemistry, and Otto Hahn was promoted to administrative director of the Kaiser Wilhelm Institute for Chemistry. Lise Meitner was also promoted to scientific associate, with the title Professor, placing her, for the first time, on an equal footing with Hahn.

James Chadwick was released from internment and returned to the Cavendish Laboratory at the University of Cambridge, England, to pursue his doctorate under Rutherford.

November 13, 1919 Stockholm, Sweden

It was announced that Fritz Haber had been awarded the 1918 Nobel Prize in Chemistry, for his method of synthesizing ammonia from its elements, nitrogen and hydrogen.

Max Planck was awarded the 1918 Nobel Prize in Physics, "in recognition of the services he rendered to the advancement of Physics by his discovery of energy quanta."

June 1, 1920 Stockholm, Sweden

Fritz Haber and Max Planck received the Nobel Prize in Chemistry and Physics respectively, in Stockholm, Sweden. The award ceremony had been delayed from the end of 1919.

September 21, 1921 7:32 am Ludwigshafen-Oppau, Germany

During the war, when sulfur was unavailable to make the ammonium sulfate needed to fix nitrogen into ammonia, the ammonia plant that Haber helped establish at Ludwigshafen-Oppau had begun making ammonium nitrate instead, despite nitrates being well-known explosives.

Two explosions, half a second apart, rocked the plant and vicinity at 7:32 am on September 21, 1921 at Silo 110, which stored 4,500 tons of a mixture of ammonium sulfate and ammonium nitrate fertilizer which formed a crater 90 m by 125 m wide and 19 m deep. The explosions were heard as far away as northeastern France and Munich. More than 500 people were killed and 2,000 more were injured.

August 7, 1922 Berlin, Germany

Lise Meitner became an official university lecturer about four years after German women in other academic fields were given the right to Habilitation. Habilitation refers to the qualification of being able to conduct self-contained university teaching.

Max von Laue wrote, in support of her belated Habilitation, "As Fräulein Meitner is one of the world's best-known scientists in radioactivity,[ii] her Habilitation is completely consistent with the interests of the faculty. I propose that she be granted permission to present a trial lecture and colloquium.... My only reason for not proposing that these be waived (on grounds of special merit) is to give her the opportunity to demonstrate her extremely thorough understanding of other fields of physics."

On August 7, 1922, Meitner delivered her Habilitation Lecture on "The Significance of Radioactivity for Cosmic Processes." A member of the academic press mistakenly referred to her lecture as having to do with "*Cosmetic* Processes."

November 9, 1922 Stockholm, Sweden

It was announced that Albert Einstein was chosen to be the recipient of the 1921 Nobel Prize in Physics.

December 10, 1922 Stockholm, Sweden

Albert Einstein was awarded the Nobel Prize in Physics "for his services to Theoretical Physics, and especially for his discovery of the law of the photoelectric effect." Einstein was not present to accept the award personally.

1923 Cambridge, England

James Chadwick stayed on as assistant director at the Cavendish Laboratory with Rutherford after earning his Ph.D. Chadwick's main research was on radioactivity. Both he and Rutherford noticed that the mass of an atom's nucleus exceeded the mass of the protons it contained. They thought that the nucleus contained additional protons that had no charge.

October 1927 Brussels, Belgium

An eminent group of physicists convened at the Fifth Solvay International Conference on Electrons and Photons in Brussels. These semiannual Solvay conferences were held in Brussels for the purpose of discussing the major open problems in physics at the time. There were related Solvay conferences that brought together top chemists. In attendance were Albert Einstein, Max Planck, Niels Bohr, Ernest Schrodinger and Werner Heisenberg, to name a few.

The discussion at hand in 1927 was the electron and the quanta. Niels Bohr had applied Planck's quantum theory to the orbits of electrons around the nucleus of an atom. However, his calculations of predicting the emitted frequencies of light given off by an atom worked only for one-electron atoms, namely hydrogen.

Physicists were scrambling to figure out how to describe the behavior of electrons in atoms. French scientist Louis de Broglie reasoned that, since light, which is a wave, can also be a particle, what if electrons, which were particles, were also waves?

Earlier that very same year, German physicist Werner Heisenberg delivered his uncertainty principle that the position of an electron and its momentum cannot be known at the same time.   And Erwin Schrodinger championed wave mechanics, a mathematical system for modeling electrons as localized wave packets, a wave-particle duality.

By the time these physicists convened at the Solvay conference of 1927, there was great debate over whose quantum theory was correct, or if the answer lied somewhere in between.

The most notable recollections of these proceedings were around a debate between Einstein and Bohr. Bohr, supported by Heisenberg, championed what became regarded as the Copenhagen interpretation. The Copenhagen interpretation went like this. Schrodinger's wave equation describes where electrons might be, but that electrons remain waves and don't exist as particles until one actually goes looking for them. In other words, electrons do not exist until they are observed.

Albert Einstein and Erwin Schrodinger on the other hand, could not wrap their heads around electrons that float in a state between existence and nonexistence. They either exist or they don't exist. Electrons are electrons, after all.

Schrodinger likened this limbo between existence and nonexistence to that of a cat in a windowless box, now famously referred to as Schrodinger's cat. Alongside the cat is a radioactive material. If the radioactive material begins to decay, then a hammer will be released which smashes a vial of poison, and kills the cat. If the radioactive substance does not decay, then the cat lives. According to the Copenhagen interpretation, the cat in the box is neither dead nor alive, but exists simultaneously as both, or neither. It is only when the box is opened that the observer perceives the cat as either alive or dead.

Though Bohr and Heisenberg eventually won the debate, Einstein was steadfastly against this probabilistic version of reality, and is noted as having commented, "I am convinced that [God] does not throw dice." To which Bohr is said to have replied, "Einstein, stop telling God what to do."

January 1932 Cambridge, England

In Germany, scientists were bombarding beryllium with alpha particles emitted by polonium. When the alpha particles hit the beryllium, beryllium emitted an unfamiliar highly penetrating radiation. Chadwick's lab duplicated the results and found that the particle given off by beryllium might possibly be that elusive neutral particle they believed added mass to the nucleus but not charge, the neutron.

To be sure, James Chadwick repeated the work of Frederic and Irene Joliot-Curie, Marie Curie's son-in-law and daughter, respectively, who aimed this as yet unfamiliar particle given off by beryllium at paraffin wax. This new particle knocked protons loose from the paraffin's hydrogen atoms, which recoiled at a very high velocity.

February 27, 1932 Cambridge, England

James Chadwick's paper "Possible Existence of a Neutron" was published in *Nature* magazine.

Franco Rasetti, a member of Enrico Fermi's lab in Italy, visited Meitner's Berlin lab to learn about radioactivity. Upon his return to Italy, he built a number of Geiger counters, and a cloud chamber modeled after Meitner's.

January 30, 1933 Berlin, Germany

In an effort to appease the Nazi party, Hindenburg appointed Adolf Hitler Chancellor of Germany.

March 10, 1933 Berlin, Germany to Pasadena, California

The first scientist to be singled out by the Nazi Party was their most famous Jew, Albert Einstein, who happened to be in California serving a guest professorship at the California Institute of Technology.

The Nazis wanted to make an example of Einstein, and began the process of publicly removing him from his professorship at the Prussian Academy. Einstein, however, refused to return to Germany. According to Einstein, "As long as I have any choice in the matter, I shall live only in a country where civil liberty, tolerance, and equality of all citizens before the law prevail."

A German publication The *Völkicsher Beobachter* published a number of attacks on Einstein, as well as did more mainstream papers. One such article titled, "Good News of Einstein - He's Not Coming Back!" referred to Einstein as "this puffed-up bit of vanity [who] dared to sit in judgment on Germany without knowing what is going on here—matters that forever must remain incomprehensible to a man who was never a German in our eyes and who declares himself to be a Jew and nothing but a Jew."

Einstein and his wife Elsa board ship to Belgium to assess the situation.

March 20, 1933 Caputh, Germany

The Nazis ransacked Einstein's summer house in Caputh, where so many scientists and dignitaries had, over the years, visited, such as Max Born, Fritz Haber, Otto Hahn, Max von Laue, Max Planck, Erwin Schrödinger, Leo Szilard, Rabindranath Tagore and Chaim Weizmann.

March 21, 1933 Ithaca, New York

Otto Hahn had been spending the spring semester as a guest lecturer at Cornell University in New York.

In her letter to Hahn of March 21, 1933, Lise described the changes to the Kaiser Wilhelm Institute already instituted by the new government.

> Dear Otto Hahn,
>
> Yesterday your 1st letter of the 10th of this month arrived and a couple of days ago the one from New York. Cordial thanks for both. I am glad that you feel comfortable on the whole in America, and I have read the beginning of your first course of lectures with pleasure, which is adapted so splendidly to American tastes. All due respect to you!
>
> Here naturally everything and everyone is affected by the radical political changes. Today is the ceremonious Reichstag inauguration in Potsdam. Last week already we had received instructions from the Kaiser Wilhelm Society to hoist the swastika flag beside the Black-White-Red imperial flag; the Kaiser Wilhelm Society is covering the cost of the flags.

The wife of Privy Councillor Schiemann and Edith [Hahn] were just here to listen to the radio broadcast of the Potsdam ceremony. It was thoroughly amicable and dignified. Hindenburg said a few short sentences and then allowed Hitler to speak, who spoke very moderately, tactfully, and personally. Hopefully things will continue in this vein. If the level-headed leaders can prevail, among whom Papen can now be counted primarily, then there is hope for developments turning out well in the end. Periods of transition almost inevitably produce all kinds of blunders, of course. Everything now depends on rational moderation.

It must surely have been difficult for Haber to have to raise the swastika flag. I was glad to hear by chance that he personally gave Kühn the directions in hoisting the brand-new flag; that is so much more dignified for him than if this requirement had been forced upon him.

Yours,

Lise

March 28, 1933 Antwerp, Belgium

Aboard ship, Albert Einstein drafted his letter of resignation to the Prussian Academy. He immediately reported upon arrival to the German Consulate in Brussels, where he hand-delivered the letter and turned in his German passport, renouncing his citizenship.

Letter of Resignation, Antwerp, March 28, 1933

To the Prussian Academy of Sciences, Berlin

The current state of affairs in Germany compel me to resign herewith from my position at the Prussian Academy of Sciences. For 19 years the Academy has given me the opportunity to devote my time to scientific research, free from all professional obligations. I know how very much I am obliged to her. I withdraw reluctantly from this circle, also because of the intellectual stimulation and the fine human relationships which I have enjoyed throughout this long period as a member and have always valued highly.

But under the present circumstances I consider my position's inherent dependence upon the Prussian government intolerable.

Respectfully yours,

Albert Einstein

March 30, 1933 Miami, Florida

Albert Einstein was so well-known and revered that his exit received worldwide attention.

Among many newspaper pieces recording Einstein's separation from Germany, the Miami Daily News-Record published this one, March 30, 1933:

Einstein to Stay Out

It was learned here last night that Prof. Albert Einstein, who has decided to remain out of Germany and who now is in Belgium, has taken steps to renounce his Prussian citizenship. Professor Einstein, who was born in Ulm, Germany, was formerly a Swiss citizen, but became a Prussian citizen in 1914 when he accepted the position in the Prussian Academy of Science.

Jews and foreign Jews in Breslau were ordered today to return all their passports to be marked as invalid for foreign travel. The object of the order, promulgated by the new police chief of Breslau, former Lieutenant Heines, is, he said, "to prevent them from circulating atrocity stories abroad."

Einstein received offers from universities from both England and the United States, among others.

Meanwhile, Lise remained at the Kaiser Wilhelm Institute in Berlin, as did most all other scientists of Jewish ancestry, hoping that the new tide of events would dissipate.

April 1, 1933 Germany

Nazi leaders call for a nationwide boycott of Jewish businesses, claiming revenge for Jews and foreigners who had criticized the Nazi regime. With Storm troopers standing guard, Jewish stars were painted on Jewish shops and signs were posted reading "Don't Buy from Jews" and "The Jews Are Our Misfortune."

The justice minister in Prussia demanded that Jewish judges step down from their posts, an ominous portent for Jewish scientists, Fritz Haber wrote concernedly to Richard Willstätter, another German chemist of Jewish descent and Nobel prize recipient.

The Prussian Academy responded to Einstein's resignation:

Prussian Academy of Sciences Press Release.

Berlin, April 1, 1933

The Prussian Academy of Sciences was shocked to learn from newspaper reports about Albert Einstein's participation in the loathesome [anti-German] campaign in America and France. It has demanded an immediate explanation from him. Einstein has since given notice of his withdrawal from the Prussian Academy of Sciences on the grounds that he could no longer serve the Prussian State under the current government. Because he is a Swiss citizen, he apparently also intends to give up his Prussian citizenship, which he had acquired in 1913 by virtue of his acceptance in the Academy as a regular full-time member.

Einstein's agitatorial behavior abroad is particularly offensive to the Prussian Academy of Sciences, because it and its members have felt intimately attached to the Prussian State since times past; and for all its strict restraint in political matters, it has always emphasized and preserved the national idea. For this reason it has no cause to regret Einstein's resignation.

For the Prussian Academy of Sciences,

Heymann

April 5, 1933 Le Coq sur Mer, Belgium

Einstein's Response, Le Coq sur Mer, April 5, 1933

To the Prussian Academy of Sciences,

I have been informed by a thoroughly reliable source that in an official statement the Academy of Sciences had alluded to Albert Einstein's participation in the loathsome [anti-German] campaign [Greuelhetze] in America and France.

I declare herewith that I have never participated in a loathsome campaign; and I must add that I have never seen any sign whatsoever of such incitement anywhere. On the whole, reports were confined to describing and commenting on the official announcements and orders by the responsible members of the German government as well as on the plans regarding the destruction of German Jews through economical means.

The statements I had given to the press relate to my resignation from my post at the Academy and to my renunciation of Prussian citizenship. I justified this on the fact that I do not wish to live in a state in which individuals are not granted equal rights before the law as well as freedom of speech and instruction. I also described the condition Germany is in today as a psychic disease afflicting the masses and also said a few things about the causes of this condition.

In a document I had given to the International League Against Anti-Semitism for publicity purposes and which was not at all intended for the press, I also called upon rational people and all those who have remained loyal to the ideals of a now threatened civilization to do their utmost to prevent the further spread of this mass-psychosis, which is expressing itself in Germany in such a terrible way. It would have been a simple matter for the Academy to acquire the correct text of my statements before commenting on me in the way it did. The German press has distorted my statements as it is prone to, which can only be expected, considering the extent to which the press is muzzled there today.

I stand behind every word I have published. On the other hand, in view of the fact that the Academy herself has been involved in slandering me before the German public, I expect that she make this statement of mine available to her members as well as to the public, before whom I have been defamed.

Very respectfully yours

Albert Einstein

April 6, 1933 Berlin, Germany

In a meeting of the Prussian Academy of Sciences, a statement was drafted to condemn Einstein, declaring that "we have no reason to regret Einstein's resignation. The Academy is aghast at his foreign agitation." Only one of the fourteen members in attendance spoke out against the condemnation, Max von Laue, who was horrified at the proceedings. Even Fritz Haber, Einstein's close friend and a Jew by birth himself, voted with the majority.

April 7, 1933 Berlin, Germany

Hitler enacts the Law for the Restoration of the Professional Civil Service, ordering the removal of all non-Aryans and others who criticize the government from civil service, including those holding positions at public universities. Non-Aryans were defined as anyone with at least one Jewish grandparent. Paul von Hindenburg, president of Germany, ensured the exemption of veterans and children of veterans of World War I.

In one day (and one decree), thirteen Nobel Prize recipients and sixty professors of theoretical physics were stripped of their positions.

The edict was announced during Easter break, when universities were empty and wouldn't reopen until the end of the month. In the meantime, Fritz Haber, the director of the Kaiser Wilhelm Institute for Chemistry, received a stack of ancestry questionnaires to be completed by his staff.

Fritz Haber would seemingly be spared from dismissal because of his service developing chemical weapons for Germany in the first World War. The fact that he had converted to Lutheranism did not exempt him from being considered Jewish. But how could he come to dismiss his own friends and colleagues, on the basis of their ancestry, an ancestry which he shared?

Haber sought advice from his friends and colleagues. Max von Laue wrote to Lise years later, recalling the conversation the three of them had:

"I remember our talks with Haber,"[iii] Laue wrote to Meitner years later, "when he sought advice and wrestled with the decision of how to deal with the different, conflicting demands from the Nazis concerning the reopening of his institute after the Easter vacation. The spiritual suffering that this great man endured is unforgettable."

Even though Lie Meitner had converted to Protestantism, she identified both her parents as Jewish on the required paperwork she completed upon returning from Easter break. For the time being, however she was still left alone to teach and do what she loved most, her research. Besides, Lise was an Austrian citizen, not German, and she and her colleagues were grasping at anything to convince themselves that Lise would remain untouched.

German students rallied around the Nazi agenda, taking the side of nationalism over their professors. Although only 1% of the German population was Jewish, Jews occupied 20% of Germany's science professorships, and 25% of physics professorships in particular.

Removing Jews from positions of authority gave nationalist Germans a much-needed relief from their supposed tyranny. After all, how was it that such a small percentage of the population could occupy such a large percentage of University professorships? Other Germans were swayed by the massive propaganda attacks on the Jews, while there was certainly more than a handful of somewhat mediocre scientists that saw this as an opportunity for their own advancement.

There were some scientists who criticized the Nazi regime, namely Fritz Strassmann, Hahn's and Meitner's assistant, and Max von Laue, who succeeded Einstein as the director of the Kaiser Wilhelm Institute in Berlin-Dahlem.

Most, however, did not speak up against the Nazis, because it was tantamount to, at a minimum, career suicide.

Besides, a hope prevailed among those left untouched that they would ultimately be spared, that German science would continue to proceed as before, and that Germans and Germany would soon return to their senses. After all, there were checks and balances in their government, and courts of law that would reestablish order and justice.
At the same time, science was an international endeavor, fueled by a healthy equilibrium of competition and collaboration. Cutting off Germany from the rest of the scientific community was the final nail in the coffin for Germany's scientific preeminence.

April 30, 1933 Berlin, Germany

After weeks of inner turmoil, Fritz Haber resigned from the Kaiser Wilhelm Institute rather than give in to the Nazi agenda and fire his beloved staff.

He wrote to the Prussian Ministry of Education:

> My decision to request retirement[iv] derives from the contrast between the research tradition in which I have lived up to now and the changed views which you, Minister, and your ministry advocate as representatives of the current large national movement.
>
> My tradition requires that in a scientific post, when choosing co-workers, I consider only the professional and personal qualifications of applicants, without considering their racial make-up. You will not expect a man in his 65th year to change a manner of thinking which has guided him for the past thirty-nine years of his life in higher education, and you will understand that the pride with which he has served his German homeland his whole life long now dictates this requirement for resignation.

He requested that he be allowed to stay until October to close out his position and find a successor.

Max Planck, the president of the Kaiser Wilhelm Society, personally appealed to the Nazi culture minister to retain Haber, to which the minister replied, "I'm finished with the Jew Haber."

May 10, 1933 Berlin, Germany

German university students, furthering the Nazi cause, met on April 6, 1933 at the Nazi German Student Association's Main Office for Press and Propaganda and declared a nationwide "Action against the Un-German Spirit," that would culminate in a massive book burning to take place the following month.

On May 10, 1933, over 25,000 "Un-German" books were burned publicly and German students marched bearing torches throughout college towns. Joseph Goebbels, the Nazi Minister for Popular Enlightenment and Propaganda, spoke that night in Berlin saying, "No to decadence and moral corruption! Yes to decency and morality in family and state! I consign to the flames the writings of Heinrich Mann, Ernst Gläser, Erich Kästner."

In addition to the works of Mann, Gläser and Kästner, authors whose works went up in flames that night included Bertolt Brecht, August Bebel, Karl Marx, Ernest Hemingway, Thomas Mann, Merich Maria Remarque, Jack London, Theodore Dreiser, Helen Keller and of course, the father of "Jewish physics," Albert Einstein.

And, added to the conflagration was a particular play by Jewish poet Heinrich Heine titled *Almansor*, containing the admonition, "Where they burn books, they will also ultimately burn people."

May 16, 1933 Berlin, Germany

Planck plead his case before Hitler himself, appealing to him that getting rid of Jewish scientists would be akin to performing scientific "self-mutilation[v]." Hitler responded that he was more concerned with the communists than the Jews, but that "Jews are all communists. A Jew is a Jew... They all cling together like burrs."

Hitler worked himself into such a fury that Planck had to leave the room. It took Planck some months to recover from this encounter.

Planck was right. Of the top scientists working on the Manhattan Project that successfully developed the atomic bomb, Leo Szilard, Enrico Fermi, Stanislaw Ulam, Eugene Wigner, Edward Teller, Hans Bethe, Emilio Segre, John von Neumann, James Franck were all refugees of fascist Europe.

May 22, 1933 England

The newly formed Academic Assistance Council, formed in England to siphon Jewish scientists out of Germany, issued the following statement:

> Official Statement of the Academic Assistance Council[vi]
>
> Many eminent scholars and men of science and University teachers of all grades and in all faculties are being obliged to relinquish their posts in the Universities of Germany.
>
> The Universities of our own and other countries will, we hope, take whatever action they can to offer employment to these men and women, as teachers and investigators. But the financial resources of Universities are limited and are subject to claims for their normal development which cannot be ignored. If the information before us is correct, effective help from outside for more than a small fraction of the teachers now likely to be condemned to want and idleness will depend on the existence of large funds specifically devoted to this purpose. It seems clear also that some organisation will be needed to act as a centre of information and put the

teachers concerned into touch with the institutions that can best help them.

We have formed ourselves accordingly into a provisional Council for these two purposes. We shall seek to raise a fund, to be used primarily, though not exclusively, in providing maintenance for displaced teachers and investigators, and finding them the chance of work in Universities and scientific institutions.

We shall place ourselves in communication both with Universities in this country and with organisations which are being formed for similar purposes in other countries, and we shall seek to provide a clearing house and centre of information for those who can take any kind of action directed to the same end. We welcome offers of co-operation from all quarters. We appeal for generous help from all who are concerned for academic freedom and the security of learning. We ask for means to prevent the waste of exceptional abilities exceptionally trained. The issue raised at the moment is not a Jewish one alone; many who have suffered or are threatened have no Jewish connection.

The issue, though raised acutely at the moment in Germany, is not confined to that country. We should like to regard any funds entrusted to us as available for University teachers and investigators of whatever country who, on grounds of religion, political opinion or race are unable to carry on their work in their own country.

Our action implies no unfriendly feelings to the people of any country; it implies no judgment on forms of government or on any political issue between countries.

Our only aims are the relief of suffering and the defence of learning and science.

Among those who helped found the Academic Assistance Council were Ernest Rutherford and Leo Szilard. The latter, a Hungarian-born Jew who had only recently in 1930 received German citizenship, had emigrated to England, noting the rising tide of anti-Semitism in Germany.

Summer 1933

Albert Einstein found that he was listed as an enemy of the state in a pamphlet circulating throughout Germany under the heading "Not Yet Hanged."

Otto Hahn would later recall in his memoirs why he and other Aryans didn't take a stronger stance to protect their non-Aryan colleagues:

"Planck (and others) advised against it: 'If today you assemble 50 such people, then tomorrow 150 others will rise up who want the positions of the former, or who in some way wish to ingratiate themselves with the Minister.' I therefore did not attempt anything."[vii]

Leo Szilard[viii], the Hungarian physicist who played a crucial role in the later Manhattan Project, remarked in later years how Hitler's rise to power had less to do with Hitler's popularity, and more to do with the absence of resistance:

> Many ... people took a very optimistic view of the situation. They all thought that civilized Germans would not stand for anything really rough happening.
>
> The reason that I took the opposite position was ... [that] I noticed that the Germans always took a utilitarian point of view. They asked, 'Well, suppose I would oppose this

thinking, what good would I do? I wouldn't do very much good, I would just lose my influence. Then why should I oppose it?'

"ou see, the moral point of view was completely absent, or very weak.... And on that basis I reached in 1931 the conclusion that Hitler would get into power, not because the forces of the Nazi revolution were so strong, but rather because I thought that there would be no resistance whatsoever.

At the same time, most German scientists retained a strong sense of German loyalty and the very same nationalism which blindly drove them into World War I. Kaiser Wilhelm Society correspondence, of which Max Planck was director, now routinely featured a swastika and the greeting "Heil Hitler."

October 17, 1933

Albert Einstein, along with his wife Elsa, his secretary Helen Dukas and assistant Walther Mayer, emigrated to the United States to assume a position at the Institute for Advanced Study at Princeton University.

Fritz Haber emigrated to England, living and working in Cambridge for a few months. There, Ernest Rutherford, who was then president of the Academic Assistance Council in England, famously refused to shake Haber's hand for the latter's role in the use of chemical warfare in World War I. At the second battle Ypres alone, 90 British troops died from gas poisoning in the trenches, 46 died soon after at the dressing stations, and 12 died after long suffering.

Chaim Weizmann, chemist and future President of Israel, offered Haber the position as director of the Daniel Sieff Research Institute in Rehovot, which was then part of Mandatory Palestine. The Daniel Sieff Research Institute would later become the Weizmann Institute.

Otto Hahn, Meitner's research partner, assumed the interim directorship of the Kaiser Wilhelm Institute in Haber's place, and following the Nazi's bidding, fired the Jews and other perceived "enemies of the state." Lise Meitner stayed on, not being German herself.

Why did she stay? The same question could be asked of hundreds of thousands of others who stayed when there was still time to leave. At least on Lise's part, she was a physicist on par with the great physicists of her generation, Einstein, Schrodinger and Planck, doing the work she loved. She earned this position of prominence amid a lifetime of societal and institutional sexism, and the idea of starting from scratch somewhere else was inconceivable. In 1947, she justified in a letter to a friend why she chose to remain: "I built it from its very first little stone; it was, so to speak, my life's work, and it seemed so terribly hard to separate myself from it."

Why did she stay? She stayed because she couldn't bear the thought of the alternative. She stayed because no one was forcing her to leave. And she stayed because she, along with most others, believed that the current spike in nationalism would pass.

September 6, 1933 Berlin, Germany

Lise Meitner's authorization to teach at the University of Berlin was rescinded, based upon the third paragraph of the Law for the Restoration of the Civil Service of 7 April 1933. The reasons given were that she was "100% non-Aryan," her military service in World War I as an X-ray technician, which would have exempted her, was not at the front, and she was not grandfathered in as her Jewish colleagues were, as she didn't achieve full professorship until 1922. Of course, the only reason she didn't achieve full professorship before 1922 was because of her gender.

Meitner was subsequently barred from scientific societies and wasn't allowed to present scientific papers. "One constantly hears essentially only my name for an investigation in which Lise Meitner has participated at least as much as I have," wrote Otto Hahn in 1936.

Naturwissenschaften became the nearly exclusive publisher of Lise's papers between the years 1933-1935. Known in English as the *Science of Nature, Naturwissenschaften,* under the editorship of Arnold Berliner, continued to publish scientific papers written by Jews, being himself a Jew. The Nazis and their scientists boycotted the journal as a result, and Berliner was finally dismissed in August 1935.

Nature magazine, upon learning of his dismissal, published the following note:

> We much regret[ix] to learn that on August 13 Dr. Arnold Berliner was removed from the editorship of *Die Naturwissenschaften*, obviously in consequence of non-Aryan policy. This well-known scientific weekly, which in its aims and features has much in common with *Nature*, was founded twenty-three years ago by Dr. Berliner, who has been the editor ever since and has devoted his whole activities to the journal, which has a high standard and under his guidance has become the recognized organ for expounding to German scientific readers subjects of interest and importance.

Berliner, as a result, fell ill and sank into a depression, during which Max von Laue proved a constant and loyal friend.

October 12, 1933 London, England

On October 12, 1933, Leo Szilard was incensed by an article he read that morning in the *Times*, quoting Ernest Rutherford talking about the energy content in an atom's nucleus:

> We might in these processes obtain very much more energy than the proton supplied, but on the average we could not expect to obtain energy in this way. It was a very poor and inefficient way of producing energy, and anyone who looked for a source of power in the transformation of the atoms was talking moonshine. But

the subject was scientifically interesting because it gave insight into the atoms.

The article motivated Szilard to go looking for "moonshine," in the form of nuclear chain reactions.

October 22-29, 1933 Brussels, Belgium

Lise Meitner attended the Seventh Solvay Conference in Belgium, the topic that year being "Structure and properties of the atomic nucleus." The focus of this conference was on the subatomic particles, most specifically, the newly discovered neutron, as well as the positron and deuteron. Also present at this meeting were Marie Curie and her daughter Irene Joliot-Curie, along with her son-in-law Frederic Joliet. While the quantum physicists were theorizing about electrons, Lise and Irene were focused on the nucleus itself.

November 25, 1933 London, England

Nature published the proceedings of the Academic Assistance Council, whose aim was to relocate and ultimately save displaced German scientists. Ernest Rutherford served as its president. Rather than avert his eyes to the political climate of Germany that would ultimately spread throughout Europe, Rutherford used his position and connections in the scientific community to help those who otherwise may have had nowhere else to go.

Nature Magazine, November 25, 1933

A meeting of the Academic Assistance Council, under the presidency of Lord Rutherford, recently reviewed the work accomplished during its first six months in assisting university teachers and investigators who, on grounds of race, religion or political opinion, are unable to carry on their work in their own countries. The Council has collected records of about one thousand displaced scientific workers and scholars. One hundred and thirty-two have been given temporary research facilities in the Universities and University Colleges of Belfast,

Birmingham, Bristol, Cambridge, Cardiff, Edinburgh, Glasgow, Hull, Leeds, London, Manchester, Nottingham and Oxford.

Among the 2,600 lesser-known refugees the Academic Assistance Council helped relocate, 16 would go on to win Nobel Prizes.

Otto Robert Frisch, Lise Meitner's nephew and fellow physicist, was one such displaced refugee. He was dismissed from his position in Hamburg, finding himself in need of the Academic Assistance Council. In late 1933 he went to London to work at Birkbeck College, and from there when to Copenhagen to work under Niels Bohr.

December 10, 1933 Stockholm, Sweden

Erwin Schrodinger, along with Paul Dirac, accept the Nobel Prize in Physics "for the discovery of new productive forms of atomic theory." Werner Heisenberg was also on hand to receive the belated 1932 Nobel Prize in Physics.

Erwin Schrodinger, fresh Nobel Prize in hand, could now go anywhere, and chose to leave Nazi Germany, although not Jewish, and not a target of the new regime. His departure, justifiably, was a blow to fellow Germans. Schrodinger emigrated first to Oxford, England, then to Princeton, New Jersey, and ultimately landed a position at the University of Graz in Austria in 1936. It is believed that this frequent change of positions was due to his unconventional behavior and living arrangement, cohabitating with his wife and pregnant mistress. Over the years, he had children with two other female students of his.

Still, Schrodinger, at the time of his departure, was the most prominent Aryan German scientist of his day.

January 11, 1934 Paris, France

Frederic Joliot was working that evening in the physics lab in the basement. He had been experimenting with the alpha decay of polonium. When radioactive polonium decays to become a more stable element, it gives off alpha particles, which consist of 2 protons and 2 neutrons, much like the nucleus of the helium atom. By placing the polonium in front of a Wilson cloud chamber, he was able to watch the alpha particles that the polonium sample gave off. Alpha particles, like all atoms, are too small to see directly, which is the genius of using a cloud chamber. A cloud chamber is a glass enclosure saturated with water or alcohol vapor. When a decay particle goes through the cloud chamber, the saturated water or alcohol condenses around it, forming a vapor track. It is the vapor track that Frederic would observe. And, since the particles moved so quickly, he would record their movement with a high-speed camera.

Joliot would then place a stable element in between the radioactive polonium source and cloud chamber. By doing so, he could observe if polonium's alpha particles went through or got stopped by the stable element.

For that evening's experiment, Frederic placed a piece of aluminum in between the polonium and the cloud chamber. The particles he would observe in the cloud chamber either came from the polonium, passing through the aluminum, or from the aluminum itself, released as a result of being bombarded by polonium's alpha particles. Frederic also employed a Geiger counter to audibly record the radioactivity.

Frederic would pull the polonium further away from the aluminum to record the effects of distance on its ability to knock particles from the aluminum. What he discovered, however, surprised him. After pulling the polonium away from the aluminum, the Geiger counter was still recording radioactivity from the stable aluminum.

Frederic concluded that the alpha particles caused the stable aluminum to become radioactive. This was the first recorded evidence of an element acquiring radioactivity.

Frederic hurried Irene down from the upstairs lab to verify his findings. They similarly enjoined a colleague to do the same. There was no doubt about it. Frederic and Irene Joliot-Curie had discovered artificial radioactivity.

The identity of every element on the Periodic Table is determined by the number of protons in its nucleus. Aluminum has an atomic number of 13, so it has 13 protons. Any element that has 13 protons in its nucleus is aluminum. Though all atoms of aluminum contain 13 protons, not all atoms of aluminum have the same number of neutrons, the neutral particle also housed in the nucleus. Atoms of aluminum that have different numbers of neutrons are known as isotopes.

When aluminum's nucleus of 13 protons absorbed an alpha particle made up of 2 protons and 2 neutrons, the aluminum's atomic number, which is equal to the number of protons in its nucleus, increased by 2. The element on the periodic table with an atomic number of 15 is phosphorus. The Joliot-Curies had made a radioactive isotope of phosphorus! Generally, phosphorus is not a radioactive element, but certain isotopes of phosphorus are radioactive if they have too many neutrons. The radioactive isotope they formed had too many neutrons in its nucleus, so, like all radioactive particles, it released particles from its nucleus until it became stable again.

They proposed the following radioactive pathway to explain their results.

Phosphorus

$$^{27}_{13}Al + {}^{4}_{2}He \rightarrow {}^{30}_{15}P + {}^{1}_{0}n$$

Aluminum   Alpha   Neutron
Particle

Aluminum acquires an alpha particle in its nucleus, becoming phosphorus-30, while simultaneously releasing a neutron.

The half-life of phosphorus-30 was only three and a half minutes, which meant that, after three and a half minutes, half of the radioactive phosphorus would have already decayed into a more stable element. So the Joliot-Curies had to work quickly to confirm that the newly radioactive aluminum was not aluminum at all, but phosphorus.

As soon as the pair irradiated the aluminum with alpha particles, Marie placed the radioactive aluminum into a stoppered vial with gas tubing, to which she added hydrochloric acid. The hydrochloric acid dissolved the aluminum giving off hydrogen gas, and turned whatever radioactive phosphorus was in the sample, into radioactive phosphorus gas. Both gases were collected via the tubing into a different container. What remained in the vial was a salt of aluminum, aluminum chloride.

$$Al(s) + HCl(aq) \rightarrow AlCl_3(aq) + H_2(g)$$

In the above equation, the symbol *s* represents solid, *aq* represents aqueous which means dissolved in water, and *g* represents gas.

Irene then tested the gases for both the presence of radioactivity, which she confirmed with a Geiger counter, and the presence of phosphorus. When the presence of both were confirmed, Irene and Frederic rushed to show Irene's mother, Marie Curie. "I will never forget the expression of intense joy[x]" on Marie's countenance when the two of them showed her their findings.

On that day, Frederic and Irene had accomplished what alchemists of old had always wanted to do, to transmute one element into another, to transform base lead into pure gold. Though, in this case, they transmuted less-precious aluminum into phosphorus, the results were the same — the nucleus had been unlocked as well as its energy within.

January 29, 1934 Basel, Switzerland

While traveling to Palestine to discuss the position at the Daniel Sieff Research Institute, Fritz Haber suffered a massive heart attack in a hotel in Basel, Switzerland, and died.

February 10, 1934 Paris, France

Irene and Frederic Joliot-Curie published their results in the scientific journal *Nature*[xi] Lise Meitner sent the two a congratulatory letter, writing: "The significance of these extraordinarily beautiful results is certainly very far-reaching[xii]."

Enrico Fermi in Italy, encouraged by the Joliot-Curie findings, decided to try bombarding particles with neutrons instead of alpha particles. He believed it would be easier for a nucleus to absorb neutrons rather than alpha particles, seeing that neutrons were neutral and therefore wouldn't be repelled by a positively-charged nucleus as the alpha particles were.

Unfortunately, neutron sources did not produce neutrons at the rate that alpha sources produced alpha particles. Rather, only a few neutrons were produced when an alpha source irradiated a light element such as beryllium.

Switching from polonium to radon gas as an alpha source drastically increased the number of neutrons given off, with which Fermi was able to attempt to irradiate a number of elements on the periodic table, starting with the smallest hydrogen up through the Joliot-Curie's aluminum. He succeeded in successfully creating artificial radioisotopes (isotopes that are radioactive) from 22 elements.

March 25, 1934 Rome, Italy

Enrico Fermi published his results in an Italian journal *La Ricerca Scientifica*, sending reprints to fellow nuclear scientists, Lise Meitner in Berlin and Niels Bohr in Copenhagen. Otto Robert Frisch, Lise Meitner's nephew, who worked in Bohr's lab, translated this and subsequent articles from the Italian. "When each new copy of the Ricerca arrived I found myself the centre of a crowd demanding instant translation of Fermi's latest discoveries. And what an exciting time it was![xiii]"

Fermi noted that each new radioisotope produced using his technique of neutron bombardment would subsequently undergo beta decay. A beta particle is a particle in the nucleus identical to an electron, but resulting from the splitting of a neutron. A neutron can split into a proton and beta particle as follows:

$$\,^{1}_{0}n \rightarrow \,^{1}_{1}p + \,^{0}_{-1}e$$

Neutron Proton Beta Particle

Notice that a beta particle, just like an electron, has a negative charge (seen in its subscript) and a relative mass of zero (as indicated in its superscript).

The significance of this was that, by absorbing a neutron and subsequently undergoing beta decay to produce a proton, they may be able to artificially make elements beyond uranium on the Periodic Table. Uranium was the heaviest known element, with an atomic number 92. If they could successfully get a uranium nucleus to absorb a neutron, that neutron could beta decay into a proton, making a new element with atomic number 93 as follows:

$$\,^{238}_{92}U + \,^{1}_{0}n \rightarrow \,^{239}_{92}U \rightarrow \,^{239}_{93}? + \,^{0}_{-1}e$$

Lise, excited by the possibilities, urged Otto Hahn to drop what he was doing and join her in the creation of new and larger atomic nuclei.

In order to do so, they too would also need a neutron source. Recall that Fermi had generated neutrons by irradiating beryllium with radon. Meanwhile, Leo Szilard had successfully generated lower-energy neutrons by irradiating beryllium with the gamma rays given off by radioactive radium. These lower-energy neutrons were more likely to be captured by nuclei than the higher-energy neutrons given off by irradiating beryllium with radon, as the Joliot-Curies had generated.

Meitner and Hahn proceeded to irradiate uranium with their slow-energy neutron source, hoping to create new elements beyond uranium, referred to as transuranic elements, or transuranes for short. They used various solubility rules to precipitate elements with atomic numbers 90, 91 and 92 from the solution, leaving behind what they hoped would be the radioactive elements number 93 and above.

They then separated these unknown transuranes from solution by precipitating them out with osmium sulfide and rhenium sulfide. When the solids they obtained had half-lives of 90 minutes and 13 minutes, Meitner and Hahn knew they had successfully isolated two "new" transuranic elements. Believing the 13-minute half-life element to be similar to rhenium, a transition metal above it in the periodic table, and the 90-minute half-life element to be similar to its corresponding transition metal osmium, these two transuranic elements were called ekarhenium and ekaosmium, respectively.

The Periodic Table was introduced in 1869 by Dmitri Mendeleev, a Russian chemist and professor. Mendeleev sorted the elements that were known to him at the time, approximately 60 of them, by ascending atomic mass and chemical and physical properties. He noticed that, when elements were ordered by mass, they exhibited a periodic similarity of properties. He identified the alkali metals, the highly reactive metals in the first column of the periodic table as having common properties, as well as the alkaline earth metals, a somewhat less reactive group of metals found in the second column of the periodic table, and the halogens, a group of reactive nonmetals found in the second to last column.

In arranging the elements, Mendeleev noticed that some heavier elements belonged earlier in the periodic table because of their properties, and he predicted the existence of some elements that had yet to be discovered as missing pieces in his periodic puzzle. His table turned out to be remarkably accurate in that those missing elements were later discovered and fit neatly where Mendeleev predicted they would. And, when scientists sorted the elements by atomic number, the number of protons in an atom's nucleus, discovered by Rutherford after Mendeleev's death, the periodicity of the elements' properties was uncanny.

It was only natural that Meitner and Hahn then would expect the properties of their new transuranic elements to match those in the columns above, hence the names ekarhenium and ekaosmium.

August 2, 1934 Poland and Germany

Paul von Hinderburg, President of Germany, died. Hitler, in turn, became president of Germany.

August 4, 1934

Hitler seized control of the Germany army.

August 19, 1934

Hitler eliminated position of President of Germany and declares himself the Führer.

January 29, 1935 Berlin, Germany

One of the last acts of German scientific resistance was the memorial service to Fritz Haber, one year after his death, arranged by Max Planck and Otto Hahn. Otto recalls:

> Planck was, however, excited and pleased that the ceremony will take place in spite of all the odds, unless perhaps on our short walk [to Harnack House] a group [of thugs] sent by the [Nazi] Party will try to prevent us from entering by force. But nothing happened … The lovely large reception hall of Harnack House … was full. … Most of those present were women, the wives of Berlin professors [or] of members of the Kaiser Wilhelm Society … They came as representatives of their husbands who had been prevented by a brutal prohibition from bidding their final farewell to an important person and scientist.

Even Max von Laue, a staunch friend of Haber's, who had just a year before defied the Nazis by publishing an obituary in *Naturwissenschaften* at the time of Haber's death, likening the Haber process of making ammonia from nitrogen gas to taking "bread from air," did not attend the memorial service.

August 2, 1935 Berlin, Germany

By this time, analytical chemist Fritz Strassmann had joined Meitner and Hahn, as the latter was consumed with the administrative responsibilities associated with being the interim director of the Kaiser Wilhelm Institute. By refusing to join the Nazi party, Strassmann had isolated himself from other scientific colleagues, and had rendered himself unemployable. In doing so, however, he was a perfect match for Lise Meitner, who was growing increasingly more isolated herself.

Hahn, Meitner and Strassmann published in *Naturwissenschaften* their discovery of the two transuranic elements ekarhenium and ekaosmium, having half-lives of 13-minutes and 90-minutes, respectively, as well as a third transuranic element with a half-life of 3.5 days.

The three of them would collaborate as follows. The two chemists Hahn and Strassmann would separate and isolate the radioactive transuranes and Meitner, the physicist, would propose the nuclear decay pathways to explain their existence. Meitner's task grew increasingly more difficult as the results they were obtaining somewhat defied what they knew about radioactive decay processes at the time. Further, with each subsequent experiment, the team focused their analyses on the radioactive transuranic solids they were able to precipitate from solution, leaving the filtrate, the remaining solution, unanalyzed and untouched.

Still, the Joliot-Curies in France, Fermi in Italy and Ernest Lawrence in Berkeley, California found similar results and reached similar conclusions.

May 17, 1935 Berlin, Germany

Meitner, Hahn and Strassmann, fearing their exhaustive research had reached a dead end, turned their attention to thorium. Thorium has an atomic number of 90, meaning it contains 2 protons fewer than uranium.

When the team irradiated thorium with slow neutrons, it was clear that the thorium nucleus captured the neutron, increasing its mass number by one. This artificially radioactive thorium had a half-life of

30 minutes, which decayed by giving off a beta particle, into protactinium-233.

$$^{232}_{90}Th + ^{1}_{0}n \rightarrow ^{233}_{90}Th \rightarrow ^{233}_{91}Pa + ^{0}_{-1}e$$

They were limited at this time by what they already had learned to be true about nuclear decay. They knew, for one, that when an isotope decayed by giving off an alpha particle, its atomic number decreased by two. Secondly, when an isotope decayed by giving off a beta particle, its atomic number increased by one. Therefore, when searching for and isolating nuclear decay products, they narrowed their search for decay products that were within one or two atomic numbers of the sample they were irradiating. Just above uranium and thorium in the periodic table were the yet-to-be-discovered transuranium elements. Just below them were protactinium, which Lise and Otto had discovered, and actinium. They never thought to look for any other elements further away.

Still, it seemed as if, to Lise Meitner at least, the pathways she mapped out to explain the decay products were quite complex and defied some of the principles she already knew to be true about nuclear decay.
Joliot-Curie's team, Fermi's team and Lawrence's team were all doing the same, trying to be first to discover a new element or a new pathway, or both.

December 1936

The 1936 Nobel Peace prize was awarded to journalist, socialist and pacifist Carl von Ossietzky, an outspoken critic of the Nazi regime. He was imprisoned in a Nazi concentration camp at the time and was not released to attend the ceremony in Sweden. Subsequently, the German government forbade Germans from accepting any future Nobel prizes.

October 10, 1937 Paris, France

The Joliot-Curies returned to experimenting with irradiating uranium. While in the past the supposed transuranium elements were selectively precipitated out of solution and tested for radioactivity, Irene decided not to precipitate them out this time. Rather, she decided to leave the transuranes in solution. In very practical ways, their experiment was not ideal. Leaving the transuranes in solution along with the uranium produced a hodge-podge of radioactivity, that was difficult to sort by source and product. Still, they were able to distinguish four isotopes with the half-lives 40-seconds, 2-minutes, 16-minutes, and 3.5 hours. This isotope with a 3.5-hour half-life had not been discovered previously, because it had never been precipitated out, always remaining in the filtrate.

The Joliot-Curies published their findings of this new isotope which they proposed was an isotope of thorium.

January 20, 1938 Berlin, Germany and Paris, France

Lise Meitner and her team repeated Irene's experiments looking for thorium in the filtrate as Irene had proposed, but did not find it. Meitner wrote to Joliot-Curie to retract her supposition that the new radioisotope with a 3.5-hour half-life was thorium, which she did.

Lise did not pursue the 3.5-hour half-life radioisotope, dismissing it as essentially bad chemistry, though perhaps she should have. Meanwhile, back in Paris, this became Irene's sole focus.

Irene managed to precipitate out the isotope, finding that it had properties very similar to those of lanthanum.

The Berlin team, looking down on the Paris team as lesser scientists with poorer technique, referred to the Joliot-Curies' 3.5-hour unidentified radioisotope as "Curiosum."

March 12, 1938 Austria

On March 12, 1938, German troops marched into Austria, in what has become known as the *Anschluss*, the annexation. Austrians welcomed the troops with cheers, flowers and Nazi salutes, which surprised even the Nazis.

Hitler himself drove over the border at his birthplace, Braunau am Inn, and arrived that evening in Linz to more cheering crowds.

Overnight, Nazi flags, arm bands, and "Heil Hitler" salutes proliferated the once independent Austria.

And overnight, the protection Meitner's Austrian citizenship provided her was gone.

March 13, 1938 Berlin, Germany

Kurt Hess, a Nazi scientist on the top floor of Lise Meitner's Kaiser Wilhelm Institute remarked, "The Jewess endangers the institute." Word of this denunciation reached Otto Hahn the next day, who subsequently confided in Lise.

March 14, 1938 Zurich, Switzerland

Paul Scherrer wrote to Lise urging her to come to Zurich.

"We will almost certainly have a Congress here this summer. In case it doesn't take place, I would like to invite you to give a lecture in any case on April 23. We have a colloquium every Wednesday from 3–5 P.M."

March 15, 1938 Vienna, Austria

In one of his most famous speeches, Hitler addressed a crowd of approximately 200,000 cheering German Austrians gathered around the Heldenplatz in Vienna, saying:

"The oldest eastern province of the German people shall be, from this point on, the newest bastion of the German Reich... As leader and chancellor of the German nation and Reich I announce to German history now the entry of my homeland into the German Reich."

March 17, 1938 Elberfeld, Germany

Hahn, worried about the future of his institute, went to discuss Meitner's situation with the treasurer of the Kaiser Wilhelm Institute.

Meanwhile, Lise visited her lawyer.

March 20, 1938 Berlin, Germany

Otto Hahn returned to the institute and informed Lise of the outcome of his meeting — she needed to leave the Institute, at once.

March 21, 1938 Berlin, Germany

Lise did not heed Hahn's instructions, returning the next day to the Institute as usual.

March 22, 1938 Berlin, Germany

March 22, 1938 marked Otto and Edith Hahn's 25th wedding anniversary. Though things were undeniably awkward between Otto and Lise, Lise tried to conduct herself as usual, visiting the couple for the customary well wishes in the morning.

That evening, Hörlein, the Institute's treasurer called Hahn to retract his directive regarding Meitner. She could stay for now. Hahn informed Lise, though the die had already been cast — she knew that Hahn was more than willing to sell her out for the sake of his position at the Institute. Even while she accompanied the anniversary couple's celebration that night, she found it increasingly difficult to hide her feelings about what she saw as Hahn's betrayal.

March 31, 1938 Berlin, Germany

Lise, accompanied by Otto, met directly with Ernst Telschow, General Director of the Kaiser-Wilhelm-Institute to discuss her status and pension, should she be dismissed.

Telschow, after consulting with Carl Bosch, then president of the Kaiser Wilhelm Institute, told her that the Institute wanted her to stay.

Stay or go. Lise wanted to stay, so Bosch's words were reassuring. And yet, who's to say that tomorrow he wouldn't change his mind, as Horlein had done, or that someone else would order her to leave?

Invitations to leave the country began trickling in, in the guise of offers to visit other laboratories, like a life preserver tossed to a drowning man. Niels Bohr, who had been active relocating displaced German scientists, sent Lise one such letter to come to Copenhagen:

> The local Physical Society and the Chemistry Association have delegated me to ask you if you would give their members the great pleasure and generous instruction by holding a seminar in the near future concerning your very fruitful investigations of the artificially induced new radioactive families of radioactive elements. As to the date, we can entirely accommodate ourselves to your convenience. It would suit us particularly well, however, if you were able to arrange to come here some time in the first half of the month of May. It goes without saying that the Physical Society and the Chemistry Association will cover all your travel expenses, and you would give my wife and me special pleasure if you would live with us during your stay in Copenhagen.

Lise did not take the life preserver, however. She wanted to stay in Berlin. And even when all signs indicated that it was time to leave, Lise clung to the one possibility that she could somehow be allowed to continue her research under Nazi rule.

April 1938 Berlin, Germany

Lise's status was now brought up before the Ministry of Education.

Lise reached out to friends and colleagues daily to keep abreast of her situation, no longer relying on often intercepted mail. In addition, she kept to her daily routines, so as not to arouse suspicion.

May 9, 1938 Berlin, Germany

Lise decided, as she wrote in her diary, that she would take Bohr up on his offer, albeit temporary, and travel to Copenhagen:

"O.R. [Otto Robert Frisch, Lise's nephew] called, whether I could come [to Copenhagen]. Said yes."

May 10, 1938 Berlin, Germany

Lise went to the Danish consulate to secure a travel visa, only to find that the *Anschluss* had rendered her Austrian passport invalid.

May 11, 1938 Berlin, Germany

Lise and Hahn asked Carl Bosch to help her get a visa or passport.

May 20, 1938

Still no progress had been made on the visa. Lise met again with Bosch who decided to write directly to the minster of the interior, Wilhelm Frick, asking for permission for her to leave Germany:

> Honorable Herr Reichsminister! Reichsminister! In my position as head of the Kaiser-Wilhelm-Gesellschaft, I have concerned myself with an assignment which, in our opinion, only you can decide. It concerns Frau Prof. Meitner, who works scientifically in the KWI for Chemistry. Frau Meitner is non-Aryan, but with the agreement of the Ministry of Culture has been permitted to work, as she possesses great scientific experience, especially in her capacity as a physicist. During continuous scientific work with Professor Hahn she has solved many large problems. Frau Meitner has Austrian citizenship. With the return of Austria she has become a [German] citizen, and it may be assumed that the question of her separation will sooner or later become acute. Because Frau Meitner is well known in international scientific circles, I regard it as desirable for the interests of the institute to make it possible to find a solution for this situation. Frau Meitner is prepared to leave at any time to assume a scientific position in another country. She has received proposals of this kind.

It is only a question of obtaining for Frau Meitner, who has an Austrian passport, notice that she may return to Germany, otherwise travel abroad for purposes of employment is impossible, or that Frau Meitner be issued a German passport. I would, honorable Herr Reichsminister, be very grateful if, in the interests of the institute and its scientific concerns, you could put me in the position of settling this situation. Heil Hitler! C. Bosch.

June 2, 1938 Baltimore, Maryland, United States

James Franck was one of the first Jewish scientists to leave Germany after the Law for Restoration of the Professional Civil Service was enacted. He had since emigrated to the United States, where he accepted positions at Johns Hopkins and then the University of Chicago. He filed an affidavit verifying that he would support Lise if she came to the United States. Lise, however, didn't want to emigrate to the U.S., even though her sister had already moved there.

June 6, 1938 The Netherlands and Berlin, Germany

Still no word about her passport. Meanwhile, Dirk and Miep Coster invited Lise to the Netherlands, to which she had to respond: "I would accept your loving invitation[xiv] without hesitation, but my situation at the moment is such that I cannot travel at all, or at least am very uncertain it would be possible."

Meanwhile, Niels Bohr and his wife arrived in Berlin and met with Lise and Peter Debye, the director of the new Kaiser Wilhelm Institute of Physics, about her situation. Debye assured them that there was no need to rush. Bohr was more skeptical and, when he returned to Copenhagen, increased his efforts to secure a place for her.

June 9, 1938 Zurich, Switzerland

Paul Scherer wrote to Lise again, nearly insisting that she come to Zurich straight away. But again, Lise could not travel without a visa, and she could not get a visa without a passport.

I return to my letter at the start of the semester in which I invited you to lecture to our colloquium or seminar. We were all very disappointed that you didn't come after you said you would....Next Friday is our last seminar about nuclear questions....So gather yourself together and come this week, by airplane it is only a short hop. You could give your lecture Wednesday or Friday, 5–7 P.M.

June 11, 1938 Netherlands

Bohr reached out to the Scandinavian countries to secure a position for Lise. Dirk Coster, who had already invited Lise to Groningen, and Adriaan Fokker in Haarlem in the Netherlands collaborated to bring Lise over. Though university positions were few and far between, there was plenty of lab space for her. Coster began a campaign reaching out to local scientists to pledge a small monthly stipend to cover Lise's basic expenses. Corresponding with Fokker, Coster wrote:

> I have given my word that if I should get the impression that there is nothing for L.M. in Holland I shall let Bohr know in a week so that he can seek help in Denmark or Sweden. But I would regret it very much if we couldn't get her to Holland.

June 14, 1938 Berlin, Germany

Word reached Lise that new restrictions forbidding travel outside of Germany were about to go into effect. Her only hope was to receive word from the Ministry of Education, which came soon after.

June 16, 1938 Berlin, Germany

On June 16, 1938, Carl Bosch relayed the following letter to Lise.

> Per instructions of the Reichsminister Dr. Frick, I may most humbly tell you, in response to your letter of the twentieth of last month, that political considerations are in effect that prevent the issuance of a passport for Frau

Prof. Meitner to travel abroad. It is considered undesirable that well-known Jews leave Germany to travel abroad where they appear to be representatives of German science, or with their names and their corresponding experience might even demonstrate their inner attitude against Germany. Surely the K.W.G. can find a way for Frau Prof. Meitner to remain in Germany even after she resigns, and if circumstances permit she can work privately in the interests of the K.W.G. This statement represents in particular the view of the Reichsführer-SS and Chief of the German Police in the Reichsministry of the Interior.

The Reichsführer-SS to which the letter referred was Heinrich Himmler, who now knew the situation regarding Lise Meitner. Anonymity perhaps would have served her better.

Lise Meitner was now officially on notice not to leave Germany.

Peter Debye, who previously thought there was no cause for alarm, wrote to Bohr about the urgency of getting her out of Germany:

I now believe it would be good if something could happen as soon as possible. Even a very modest offer would be considered and followed up if only it provides the possibility to work and to live. That is how the situation was represented to me, and it was emphasized that a poorer but earlier offer would be preferred over one that is better but later.

June 17, 1938 Switzerland

Scherrer reached out to Meitner again, responding to the urgency of her situation:

"ARE YOU COMING FORA "PHYSICS WEEK"? 29 JUNE TO 1 JULY."

But without a passport, Switzerland was out of the question.

June 21, 1938 Copenhagen, Denmark

Niels Bohr wrote to Adriaan Fokker in the Netherlands, requiring a definitive answer as to whether there was place for Lise there, citing that there were no options for her in Copenhagen, as they were already saturated with foreign scientists.

Bohr floated the possibility that Lise could go to Sweden and work in Manne Siegbahn's institute, though "the possibilities there are only small, and it will therefore be most desirable if you and Coster continue your endeavours in Holland without delay."

Though Fokker and Coster had been gathering pledges to fund a position for Lise, they still came up short. Further, they now had to petition the Minister of Education of the Netherlands directly to make a special allowance for Lise's immigration, as the Netherlands too had become oversaturated with refugees.

Few people truly believed that Lise's situation was as desperate as we now know it was, looking back from this side of history. Even Fokker and Coster, who had only managed to secure her one year's salary, began to believe that Lise would be better off remaining in Germany. After all, even if she were dismissed, she would still have her pension, which she would most likely have to sacrifice if she emigrated.

Fokker and Coster wrote to Bohr that they had secured only one year's salary. Not receiving a reply, Coster, especially nervous about Lise's situation in Germany, decided to travel to Germany himself to assess the situation, and, if necessary, personally take her out of the country. Fokker warned him not to be too hasty. "There is no axiom that says you must bring L.M. to me. Also you must let her calmly make the decision herself."

June 27, 1938 Berlin, Germany

Dirk Coster's notice of impending arrival arrived the day that Max von Laue, Peter Debye, Ebbe Rasmussen and Lise Meitner met in Debye's home with a new offer. Rasmussen, an associate of Bohr's in Copenhagen, had offered Lise a chance to do research in Manne

Siegbahn's new institute in Stockholm, Sweden, devoted exclusively to nuclear physics.

Weighing the two options, Meitner decided to go to Sweden. Though she had fewer connections in Sweden, the chance to build a nuclear physics program from scratch appealed to her.

Peter Debye wrote back to Fokker:

> I regret, actually, that I must write that in the end Stockholm won. I would have preferred that it be Groningen, but I let myself be persuaded by the assistant himself, who thinks he will be able to accomplish more in Stockholm.... Of course I still let him know this morning what was in your letter.

The "male" assistant to which they were referring was Lise Meitner, whose identity was concealed in correspondence so as not to alert the authorities, especially after she had been expressly forbidden to leave Germany.

Fokker and Coster informed the donors that their most generous donations would not be needed after all.

Still, an unsettling letter arrived from Bohr informing the Berlin contingent that Lise's passage to Sweden had yet to be secure, as they had still not received permission from the Swedish government.

July 4, 1938 Berlin, Germany

Carl Bosch learned that the German borders were about to be sealed off to German scientists, not allowing Lise to leave. The time was now to act and leave Germany.

July 6, 1938 Berlin, Germany and Evian, France

With Sweden's borders still closed to her, and the only open invitation to the Netherlands, Peter Debye wrote back to Coster:

The assistant we talked about, who had made what seemed like a firm decision, sought me out once again....He is now completely convinced (this has happened in the last few days) that he would rather go to Groningen, indeed that this is the only avenue open to him. He intends to keep his agreement with Rasmussen, but that is only in the future; under no circumstances can he start there right away.

Delegates from thirty-two countries converged on the resort town of Evian, France to address the refugee crisis. The conference lasted for ten days. Though the countries expressed sympathy for the plight of the refugees, the only country to actually ease their immigration restrictions was the Dominican Republic. Adding to his jubilant reception in Austria, Hitler took this as confirmation that no one else wanted the Jews either, ultimately paving the way for the Final Solution.

Saturday July 9, 1938 Groningen, Netherlands and Berlin, Germany

Dirk Coster received Debye's letter. Meanwhile Lise had herself inquired about the status of her passport to find that again, her German passport was denied.

Coster replied to Debye, "I am coming to look over the assistant and if he suits me I will take him back with me."

It being Saturday, and Lise's passage to the Netherlands having yet to be secured, everyone waited anxiously for Monday.

Monday July 11, 1938 Groningen, Netherlands and Berlin, Germany

Dirk Coster received word that Lise would be welcomed into the Netherlands. Coster set out immediately for Berlin to take Lise back with him.

Meanwhile, those in Berlin waited without word. A letter wouldn't arrive in time, and would most likely be intercepted anyway, as would a telegram.

On the way to Berlin, Coster approached the immigration officers at the German-Netherlands border at Nieuwe Schans. It was believed that this lightly traveled route would be the safest way to abduct Lise out of Germany, but Coster wasn't taking any chances.

That evening, Coster arrived in Berlin and stayed at the home of Peter Debye.

Tuesday July 12, 1938 Berlin, Germany

Lise Meitner went to work at the Institute as usual. She worked until 8 o'clock that night, correcting a paper that one of her young associates was preparing for submission. Otto Hahn went home with her, helping her pack a few of her belongings. While they were saying their goodbyes, Hahn slipped her his mother's diamond ring. "Keep this. You may need it."

Hahn wrote later in his autobiography, My Life:

> We agreed on a code-telegram in which we would be let known whether the journey ended in success or failure. The danger consisted in the SS's repeated passport control of trains crossing the frontier. People trying to leave Germany were always being arrested on the train and brought back... We were shaking with fear whether she would get through or not.

Lise said goodbye to no one else, her excursion that night cloaked in utmost secrecy.

Paul Rosbaud drove her to the train station. A scientific publisher who had successfully relocated his own Jewish wife and daughter to England, Paul served as an Allied spy, using his influential position in the scientific community to gather German scientific intelligence. Though he would help many Jewish families escape Germany, Lise Meitner's would be his most famous. As they drove closer to the train station, Meitner, consumed with the fear of being caught, and the regret of leaving the only life she had known, begged Paul to take her back, to no avail.

Dirk Coster was already on the train when Lise boarded. They greeted each other as if by chance. The train ride was pleasant enough, but with all her belongings reduced to two suitcases, and her destination unconfirmed, Lise was palpably upset. That upset quickly changed to heart-pounding fear, as Lise's train approached the Dutch border. Would she be arrested? Or worse? Coster quietly took possession of the diamond ring, just in case. They crossed without incident.

Once in Groningen, Coster telegrammed Hahn that the "baby" had arrived, to which Hahn replied, "Heartiest congratulations. I was of course very happy about the news, as we were somewhat worried lately." The worry about which he wrote was that the chemist Kurt Hess, Meitner's Kaiser Wilhelm Institute adversary, had alerted the authorities that she was about to run. Few knew how narrowly Lise had escaped.

Coster was congratulated by scientists around the world. One telegram from Linus Pauling read:

"You have made yourself as famous for the abduction of Lise Meitner as for [the discovery of] Hafnium."

"I left Germany forever - with 10 marks in my purse," Lise Meitner would later write. And Hahn's diamond ring.
After she arrived safely in Groningen, Max von Laue informed her of how close a call it was:

"The shot that was to bring you down in the last minute missed you. You yourself probably did not notice it. The more so because of it, I waited for news that you had arrived safely."

July 15, 1938 Groningen, Netherlands

Lise stayed with the Coster's in Groningen, where she received word that Sweden had not yet given her permission to enter. Coster and Fokker felt responsible for her, as they had already stopped collecting funds for her to remain in the Netherlands. They pushed Siegbahn to see what he could do to help Lise immigrate.

July 21, 1938 The Netherlands

Lise learned that she would be admitted to Sweden, so she left Groningen to stay with Fokker in Haarlem, to be closer to the ports. It was only then that Fokker discovered that Sweden would admit her under one of two conditions — that she either had a German passport, or that her Austrian passport was accompanied with permission to return to German — neither of which Lise was in a position to obtain.

Lise returned to Groningen.

Fokker reached out to Siegbahn to see what else he could do.

July 26, 1938 Groningen, Netherlands to Copenhagen, Denmark

Lise was informed that she was granted a Swedish visa without restrictions.

With financial help from Coster, Lise first "flew with hidden money to Copenhagen ... fearful the whole time what would happen to me if the airplane should be forced to land in Germany," Lise wrote later.

She arrived successfully in Copenhagen, fortunately, and spent time there with Niels Bohr and her nephew Otto Robert Frisch.

August 1, 1938 Sweden

Lise left by train to Sweden, staying with her friend Eva von Bahr-Bergius in Kungälv, Sweden until September.

Lise's departure from Germany was cloaked in secrecy. Otto Hahn and perpetrated the story that she was visiting Vienna. Not conspicuously absent from the Institute, as it was still summer vacation, few knew that Lise was gone for good.

That same month, the German Ministry of Education moved to formally dismiss her.

August 17, 1938 Berlin, Germany

Germany passed its Law on Alteration of Family and Personal Names which required all Jews who had "non-Jewish" first names to adopt the additional name "Israel" for men, and "Sara" for women. Lise's lawyer officially changed Lise's name to Lise Sara Meitner.

August 29, 1938 Berlin, Germany

Otto Hahn informed his team at the Kaiser Wilhelm Institute in Dahlem of Lise's departure. Writing to Lise about their reactions, he relayed the comment of one of Lise's students that perhaps she had lost her nerve, to which Lise wrote back:

> If Flammersfeld asks[xv] whether I have lost my nerve, it is because he thinks I have abandoned my responsibilities. Why is it not frankly said that the ministry and Dr. Telschow proposed three weeks ago that I take a leave of absence? ... And Hähnchen, this overly hasty Totenfeier (memorial service) for me, before my resignation is even in effect—what could that mean for those people who were perhaps somewhat attached to me? They must surely think I evaded my responsibilities if you do not explicitly tell them it was impossible for me to stay.... My future is cut off, shall the past also be taken from me? ... I have done nothing wrong, why should I suddenly be treated like a nonperson, or worse, someone who is buried alive? Everything is hard enough as it is.

September 1938 Stockholm, Sweden

Lise began work at the new the Nobel Institute for Experimental Physics, overlooking the Royal Swedish Academy of Sciences. She was shocked to find out that, rather than being a bustling center of scientific research, the new institute was mostly empty and unequipped, and she was left to fend for herself.

She was given the salary of a research assistant, and the director of the Physics Department of the new Nobel Institute Manne Siegbahn, treated her as if she were invisible.

September 25, 1938 Stockholm, Sweden

She wrote to Hahn:

> Perhaps you cannot fully appreciate how unhappy it makes me to realize that you always think that I am unfair and embittered, and that you also say so to other people. If you think it over, it cannot be difficult to understand what it means that I have none of my scientific equipment. For me that is much harder than everything else. But I am really not embittered—it is just that I see no real purpose in my life at the moment and I am very lonely ... Work can hardly be thought of. There is [no equipment] for doing experiments, and in the entire building just four young physicists and very bureaucratic working rules.

Lise tried with limited success to get her things sent from Berlin. She was even less successful in liquidating her bank account and her pension. Her flight had sacrificed everything she had and worked for. She had nothing left to her name, and was now starting over at the age of fifty-nine.

September 8, 1938 Austria
Ernest Schrodinger was dismissed from his position at the University of Graz in Austria, because of his vocal opposition to Nazi Germany.

September 29, 1938

Italy, Great Britain and France joined with Germany in signing the Munich Agreement, dismembering Czechoslovakia in order to ward off a German invasion.

October 5, 1938 Germany

Germany Jews were forced to surrender their passports in exchange for passports with the red letter "J" stamped on them.

Asked to lecture on neutron irradiation of uranium and thorium, Lise called on Hahn to catch her up on their current separation techniques. Specifically, in a letter dated October 23, she asked Hahn, "Do you believe in the 3.5h substance?" — the same substance that she and her team had dubbed "Curiosum."

Cut off from all nuclear physics at the time, Lise was unaware of the recent publication of the Joliot-Curie and Savitch group in France. Not only did they continue to explore this radioisotope with a 3.5-hour half-life, but they had provided decay curves in their latest journal article. The Curies saw this new 3.5-hour substance as a new transurane, meaning it had a higher atomic number than uranium, though they did not have sufficient evidence to support this. On the contrary, it seemed to them that their new substance had properties more similar to the Lanthanides than the Actinides.

The Lanthanides are those elements on the Periodic Table, from atomic number 57 through 71, that are listed in a row at the bottom of the Periodic Table, just above the Actinides. Since uranium was an actinide, any transurane would be in the same row, making it an actinide as well. It went against everything the Paris lab knew to have discovered a lanthanide with the properties of an actinide.

Fritz Strassmann was intrigued by their decay graphs, however, and decided to replicate their experiments himself. He was able to isolate the 3.5-hour substance to find that its beta decay was relatively strong. Why had they not discovered this activity previously? First of all, they were looking in the precipitate, not the filtrate. Secondly, when they did decide to search the filtrate, they were only looking for thorium. They now believed that this 3.5-hour substance might possibly be an isotope of radium, produced from two subsequent emissions of alpha particles from uranium.

$$^{238}_{92}U + {}^{1}_{0}n \rightarrow {}^{235}_{90}Th + {}^{4}_{2}He \rightarrow {}^{231}_{88}Ra + {}^{4}_{2}He$$

October 18, 1938 Oxford, England

Annemarie Schrodinger, Ernest Schrodinger's wife, wrote to Lise about their narrow escape from Austria.

> Our "trip" was highly dramatic[xvi], as it coincided exactly with the height of the political crisis…. Completely unaware, we returned [from vacation] to Graz on September 8 and discovered that Erwin had been dismissed…. Erwin went to Vienna to talk to the ministry. During their talk, Erwin was asked, "Tell me, do you still have your passport?" Erwin remained completely quiet, but you can imagine that at this instant he realized what must be done. It was clear to him that it was only because of some bureaucratic mistake that we still had our passports. We wasted no time. On September 14 we went to Rome with three small suitcases, just as if we were going to Rome on a pleasure trip. Italy was the only country which did not require a visa, and in Rome other embassies were available. We shall never forget the friendship, admiration, and help we received! Soon we had all the visas we needed and went to Switzerland on the 22d. As the political situation became more and more critical, we wanted to get to England as quickly as possible before the outbreak of war. So on the critical night of September 27 to 28 we traveled from Zurich to England. There was a blackout in Switzerland. On the other side of the Rhine one could see the bright lights of Germany. Trains were overflowing … and greatly delayed. In France we passed airports with countless airplanes standing ready. All bridges and tunnels were under military guard…. Then in England in Hyde Park bomb shelters were being feverishly prepared, anti-aircraft guns pointed to the sky, everyone had gas masks. … In Paddington we heard reports of the Four Power

Conference [in Munich]. That day 80,000 children were evacuated! On the 28th we reached Oxford.

November 8, 1938 Berlin, Germany

As Hahn wrote in their November 8th letter to *Naturwissenschaften*, the creation of radium-231 from the alpha emission of thorium-235 was the first instance of alpha particle decay brought on by slow, rather than fast, neutrons.

November 9, 1938 Vienna, Austria and throughout Germany

The next evening, while Otto Hahn was enjoying dinner with Lise's sister and brother-in-law in Vienna, a nationwide pogrom was exacted on Germany's Jewish population, remembered as *Kristallnacht*, the night of broken glass. Synagogues, Jewish homes and Jewish shops were broken into, burned and vandalized. In addition, at least 91 Jews were killed and many more Jews were rounded up and arrested.

Otto, returning to Berlin after dinner, was unaware that Lise's brother-in-law Jutz Frisch was arrested that night and sent to Dachau concentration camp.

November 10, 1938 Copenhagen, Denmark

Lise arrived in Copenhagen for much-needed recreation and a dose of scientific research, the kind her isolation in Siegbahn's institute prevented her from doing. She was excited that Hahn was going to join her there as well.

November 13, 1938 Copenhagen, Denmark to Berlin, Germany

Otto Hahn arrived in Copenhagen. They talked physics all day and saw Hahn off at the train station the following morning. Both Lise and Bohr were skeptical of the Berlin lab's 3.5-hour findings, finding it hard to believe that uranium decayed along 16 separate nuclear pathways. Usually, an unstable nucleus undergoes only one type of decay. Perhaps it could be forced to undergo another type of decay if one changes the irradiation substance or technique. But 16 different pathways?

It also defied logic, and their previous research, that a slow neutron could do all that. When they previously had irradiated thorium with slow neutrons, it resulted in thorium capturing that neutron, as shown below:

$$^{232}_{90}Th + ^{1}_{0}n \rightarrow ^{233}_{90}Th \rightarrow ^{233}_{91}Pa + ^{0}_{-1}e$$

When they irradiated thorium with fast high-energy neutrons they had been able to expel an alpha particle from its nucleus. How could they possibly have been able to obtain alpha particle decay when irradiating thorium with slow neutrons, when thorium was known to capture that slow neutron? Further, how could they have obtained two subsequent alpha particle emissions from these slow neutrons.

These two subsequent alpha emissions of uranium would look like this:

$$^{235}_{92}U + ^{1}_{0}n \rightarrow ^{232}_{90}Th + ^{4}_{2}He$$
$$^{232}_{90}Th \rightarrow ^{228}_{88}Ra + ^{4}_{2}He$$

Uranium would capture a neutron and then undergo alpha decay, yielding thorium. Thorium would then undergo another alpha decay to yield radium.

Lise advised Hahn to go back and redo their experiments and identify the products definitively. To do so, they would have to isolate each decay product and plot its decay curve. After all, each isotope behaved identically with each other in all ways but in their half-lives.

Hahn returned to Germany with Lise's directive, which he communicated to Strassmann, but no one else. Hahn's position at the Kaiser Wilhelm Institute was insecure enough, having not adopted membership into the Nazi Party, without disclosing his meeting with the now-dismissed Jewess Meitner.

"In any case (according to a statement from O. Hahn) she urgently requested that these experiments be scrutinized very carefully and intensively one more time…. Fortunately L. Meitner's opinion and judgment carried so much weight with us in Berlin that the necessary control experiments were immediately undertaken," Fritz Strassmann would later recall in his [xvii].

"To this day I remain convinced that it was L. Meitner's critical demand that motivated us to test our findings once again, after which the result came to us," Strassmann continued.

Lise tried, with Hahn's help, to obtain an Swedish immigration visa for Jutz and her sister Gusti.

December 5, 1938 Stockholm, Sweden

Lise wrote to Hahn: "I often feel like a wound-up puppet that does certain things, gives a friendly smile, and has no real life in itself."

December 10, 1938 Stockholm, Sweden

Enrico Fermi arrived in Stockholm to accept the 1938 Nobel Prize in Physics "for his demonstrations of the existence of new radioactive elements produced by neutron irradiation, and for his related discovery of nuclear reactions brought about by slow neutrons."

The conferring of the Nobel Prize on Fermi was a culmination of all the work that had been done thus far on transmutation of elements into other elements. This work was being carried out simultaneously in his laboratory in Italy, in the Joliot-Curie's laboratory in France, in Hahn and Meitner's laboratory in Berlin, and at Lawrence's laboratory in Berkeley.

The presentation ceremony and Fermi's acceptance speech summed up the research that had been carried out in the first 38 years of the twentieth century in determining the essence of the nucleus, the small positive center of the atom that contains both its protons and neutrons. Most significantly, it heralded Enrico Fermi and his lab as the first group to definitively create two transuranium elements, with atomic numbers 93 and 94 just beyond uranium on the periodic table, with names Ausenium and Hesperium, respectively.

It wasn't too long before that the nucleus containing protons was discovered by Ernest Rutherford in 1911. James Chadwick, while working in Rutherford's lab, definitively identified the existence of additional neutral particles in the nucleus, as heavy as protons, known as neutrons. All atoms of the same element had the same number of protons. Most atoms of the same element had the same number of neutrons. Some atoms of the same element, however, had different numbers of neutrons. These were called isotopes. Some of these isotopes were radioactive. In other words, they were unstable and therefore decayed by giving off radioactivity in order to become stable.

Henri Becquerel had discovered in 1892 that uranium gave off strong radiation. Researching this radiation showed that it consisted of high speed alpha particles, which were helium nuclei containing two protons and two neutrons. The subsequent elements produced by giving off alpha particles — in this case, thorium with an atomic number of 90, two less than uranium's atomic number — also emitted alpha radiation until the final product was stable lead, atomic number 82. It was clear that most radiation, given off from unstable isotopes in the process of becoming stable, consisted of pieces of an atom's nucleus.

Marie Curie was successful in isolating one of these decay products, a precursor to stable lead, known as radium, atomic number 88. Later on, it was shown that the same activity could be produced from thorium and actinium. All three of these isotopes ultimately stabilized into different isotopes of lead at the end of their radioactive pathways.

With regard to lightweight elements, Ernest Rutherford was able to show how these too, when irradiated with fast high-energy alpha particles, transmuted to other atoms. He was able to successfully transform nitrogen into oxygen.

$$^{14}_{7}N + ^{4}_{2}He \rightarrow ^{17}_{8}O + ^{1}_{1}H$$

The Joliot-Curies elaborated on Rutherford's experiments, learning that the isotopes created by the alpha irradiation of lightweight particles were radioactive themselves, and therefore decayed further. This discovery was crucial, as creating artificial radioisotopes could replace their dependency on difficult-to-obtain radium.

However, this process worked only on lightweight elements with atomic numbers 20 and below.

It was Enrico Fermi who successfully irradiated heavier elements by firing neutrons at them, rather than protons. Being electrically neutral, neutrons were more capable than protons of being absorbed by the nuclei of larger atoms, not needing to overcome the electrical repulsion that protons experienced.

Initially, neutrons were obtained by mixing beryllium with a radioactive substance, such as irradiating beryllium with radon, as the Joliot-Curies had done. Later, high energy neutrons were obtained by bombarding beryllium or lithium with heavy-hydrogen nuclei.

These high energy neutrons would knock out alpha particles from lighter elements, but would be successfully absorbed by heavier elements. These heavier elements would, upon absorption of a neutron, become artificially radioactive, giving off decay products until their nuclei stabilized.

By passing these high energy neutrons through paraffin or water, they successively slowed down enough to be captured by all elements, even the light ones, with the exception of the lightest two, hydrogen and helium.
When uranium, the last element of the periodic table at the time, would absorb one of these slow neutrons, it would decay by giving off a beta particle.

$$^{235}_{92}U + ^{1}_{0}n \rightarrow ^{236}_{92}U \rightarrow ^{236}_{93}? + ^{0}_{-1}e$$

The result of this decay was the creation of a new element, with atomic number 93, which Fermi and his team dubbed Ausenium, and element 94, Hesperium.

From the ceremonies in Stockholm, Enrico Fermi and his Jewish wife Laura, emigrated to the United States, seeking permanent asylum, never to return to Italy.

Laura remarked in her autobiography how worried and tired Lise had seemed during their Stockholm visit.

December 19, 1938 Berlin, Germany

Otto Hahn wrote to Lise about their new findings. Spurred by Lise's directive in their secret Copenhagen meeting the previous month, Hahn and Strassmann, with the help of a new lab assistant, worked tirelessly to isolate and identify the decay products. They were able to separate each and every one of them and plot their decay curves, except for one, which was terribly difficult to separate from barium.

The technique of fractionation, of separating a small amount of an isotope at of a time was credited to Marie Curie in her painstaking efforts to obtain polonium and radium samples. Otto Hahn had developed this technique to perfection.

> 19.12.38 Monday eve. in the lab.
>
> Dear Lise!... It is now just 11 P.M.; at 11:45 Strassmann is coming back so that I can eventually go home. Actually there is something about the 'radium isotopes' that is so remarkable that for now we are telling only you. The half-lives of the three isotopes have been determined quite exactly, they can be separated from all elements except barium, all reactions are consistent [with radium]. Only one is not—unless there are very unusual coincidences: the fractionation doesn't work. Our Ra isotopes act like Ba.

Perhaps you can suggest some fantastic explanation. We understand that it really can't break up into barium ... So try to think of some other possibility. Barium isotopes with much higher atomic weights than 137? If you can think of anything that might be publishable, then the three of us would be together in this work after all. We don't believe this is foolishness or that contaminations are playing tricks on us.

December 21,1938 Stockholm Sweden

Lise replied to Otto:

Your radium results[xviii] are very amazing. A process that works with slow neutrons and leads to barium! ... To me for the time being the hypothesis of such an extensive burst seems very difficult to accept, but we have experienced so many surprises in nuclear physics that one cannot say without hesitation of anything: "It's impossible."

Leaving on Friday to spend Christmas in Kungälv with Eva von Bahr-Bergius, Lise told Otto to send his next correspondence there.

Hahn and Strassmann, back in the lab, verified their results. They indeed had found barium in the filtrate. Hahn wrote back to Meitner to come up with a pathway to explain their results, not realizing that she had already departed for the holiday:

We cannot hush up the results[xix], even though they may be absurd in physical terms. You can see that you will be performing a good deed if you find an alternative [explanation]. When we finish tomorrow or the day after I will send you a copy of the manuscript ... The whole thing is not very well suited for *Naturwissenschaften*. But they will publish it quickly.

December 23, 1938 Kungälv, Sweden

Lise left for Kungälv to stay with her friend Eva von Bahr-Bergius. Her nephew Otto Robert Frisch would join her there from Copenhagen.

December 29, 1938 Berlin, Germany

Hahn, too impatient to wait for Lise, went ahead and published his results in *Naturwissenschaften*.

Even in his *Naturwissenschaften* article, though, Hahn delivered his findings somewhat apologetically:

> From these experiments[xx], we must, as chemists, rename the elements in the above scheme, and instead of radium, actinium, and thorium, write barium, lanthanum, and cerium. As 'nuclear chemists' who are somewhat related to physicists, we cannot yet decide to take this big step, which contradicts all previous experiences of nuclear physics. It is still possible that we could have been misled by an unusual series of accidents.

December 24, 1938 Kungälv, Sweden

Lise, still pondering Hahn's correspondence about the barium in the filtrate, gave his December 19th letter to Frisch for his opinion.

Frisch recalled in later in his autobiography *What Little I Remember*:

> When I came out of my hotel room[xxi] after my first night in Kungälv, I found Lise Meitner studying a letter from Hahn and obviously very puzzled by it. I wanted to discuss with her a new experiment that I was planning, but she wouldn't listen; I had to read that letter. Its content was indeed so startling that I was at first inclined to be skeptical. Hahn and Strassmann had found that those three substances were not radium … [but] barium.

The suggestion that they might after all have made a mistake was waved aside by Lise Meitner; Hahn was too good a chemist for that, she assured me.... We walked up and down in the snow, I on skis and she on foot (she said and proved that she could get along just as fast that way), and gradually the idea took shape that this was no chipping or cracking of the nucleus but rather a process to be explained by Bohr's idea that the nucleus is like a liquid drop; such a drop might elongate and divide itself.... We knew that there were strong forces that would resist such a process, just as the surface tension of an ordinary liquid drop resists its division into two smaller ones. But nuclei differed from ordinary drops in one important way: they were electrically charged, and this was known to diminish the effect of the surface tension.

At this point we both sat down on a tree trunk, and started to calculate on scraps of paper. The charge of a uranium nucleus, we found, was indeed large enough to destroy the effect of surface tension almost completely; so the uranium nucleus might indeed be a very wobbly, unstable drop, ready to divide itself at the slightest provocation (such as the impact of a neutron).

But there was another problem. When the two drops separated they would be driven apart by their mutual electric repulsion and would acquire a very large energy, about 200 MeV in all; where could that energy come from? Fortunately Lise Meitner remembered how to compute the masses of nuclei from the so-called packing fraction formula, and in that way she worked out that the two nuclei formed by the division of a uranium nucleus would be lighter than the original uranium nucleus by about one-fifth the mass of a proton. Now whenever mass disappears energy is created, according to Einstein's formula $E = mc^2$, and one-fifth of a proton mass was just equivalent to 200 MeV. So here was the source for that energy; it all fitted!

What Hahn and Strassmann accomplished in the laboratory, Lise explained as follows. Uranium had 92 protons, barium only 56. Up until this point, nuclear physicists had only been aware of radioactive nuclei giving off small particles such as alpha particles or beta particles, causing them to transmute into a neighboring element. For a nucleus to go from 92 protons to 56 protons required a literal splitting of the atom.

Uranium-235, when irradiated with a neutron, would capture that neutron and then split into two smaller halves, barium-144 and krypton-91, as shown here:

$$^{235}_{92}U + ^{1}_{0}n \rightarrow ^{144}_{56}Ba + ^{91}_{36}Kr$$

Other uranium-235 nuclei split into cesium and rubidium. This explained why the Joliot-Curies identified so many different nuclei in their experiments. Further, all those transuranes that they had thought they discovered over the past four years, including the transuranes for which Fermi was conferred the Nobel prize, ausenium and hesperium, may have been lighter elements incorrectly identified after all.

Lise realized right away what Hahn had unearthed in the laboratory. It would change the course of physics forever, and, in the short term, it would change the course of the war.

January 2-3, 1939 Copenhagen, Denmark to New York, New York

Frisch returned to Copenhagen with news of the discovery of nuclear fission, the splitting of the atom into two halves.

> Dear Tanterl[xxii], I was able to speak with Bohr only today about the splitting of uranium. The conversation lasted only five minutes as Bohr agreed with us immediately

about everything. He just couldn't imagine why he hadn't thought of this before, as it is such a direct consequence of the current concept of nuclear structure. He agreed with us completely that this splitting of a heavy nucleus into two big pieces is practically a classical phenomenon, which does not occur at all below a certain energy, but goes readily above it.

Niels Bohr, on his way to the U.S., took the news with him, though he promised not to talk about it until Frisch and Leitner published their findings.

Frisch conducted his own verification experiments to publish along with their February paper.

Meanwhile, the Fermi's arrived in New York City. Given many job offers, Enrico accepted a position as Professor of Physics at Columbia University.

January 6, 1939 Berlin, Germany

Hahn and Strassmann's paper was published in *Naturwissenschaften*, making public the discovery of nuclear fission, which wasn't named as such until Meitner and Frisch's paper in *Nature* the following month.

Because of the Nazi regime, Hahn could never have included Lise's name as a co-contributor of this article, nor as a collaborator. The fact that the two of them still remained in contact was dangerous enough, especially as there were plenty of mediocre Nazi scientists at the Kaiser Wilhelm Institute perched over the carrion of their non-loyalist colleagues.

Hahn's distancing from Meitner began last year when he learned that her presence was jeopardizing his own position. Though unintentional, the timing and exclusion of Meitner from this seminal paper distanced himself even further.

When his paper was received with cheers and adulation, he realized that fission would secure his position at the Institute, like a "gift from heaven[xxiii]." Over the next couple of months, however, he began to believe the hype that he had been selling, that fission was his discovery, his and his alone.

January 7, 1939 *Drottningholm*, en route to New York

Though Bohr had given his word not to disseminate Meitner and Frisch's findings, it was a long voyage across the Atlantic, and Bohr went over the physics again and again in the company of fellow traveler and physicist Leon Rosenfeld. He forgot to tell Rosenfeld to keep quiet, so that, by the time Hahn and Strassmann's article had been published in America, physicists were already clamoring to replicate the fission experiments.

It was a great race to see who came in first, and while Meitner and Frisch were taking their time with publishing their *Nature* piece — Frisch wanted to take the necessary time to verify his results in the laboratory — Bohr was trying to keep the lid clamped down on the metaphorical Pandora's box as it were. Bohr kept impatiently writing to Frisch asking him when the article would be sent to the publishers. Meanwhile, the word was out.

"Rosenfeld described to me[xxiv] the scene he and Bohr witnessed: a physicist simultaneously … recording fragments … and phoning to an anxious newspaperman: 'Now, there's another one'," wrote Frisch in his *Interest is Focussing*.

"Enrico [Fermi] picked the work up[xxv] when he heard about the discovery of fission, because fission explained what he had done in Rome and what they had not understood was going on," wrote his wife Laura in her book *Atoms in the Family*.

January 14, 1939 Stockholm, Sweden

Lise received word that her sister and brother-in-law Gusti and Jutz Frisch had obtained a Swedish visa and that Jutz would be released from Dachau and come to Stockholm.

February 4, 1939 Stockholm, Sweden

Lise wrote to Hahn:

> With me things are not good at all[xxvi]. I have a place to
> work here but no position that gives me the least right to
> anything. Try for a moment to imagine how it would be if
> instead of your own beautiful institute, you had one
> work room in a strange institute, without the slightest
> help, without any rights, and with Siegbahn's attitude: he
> only loves big machines, is very sure of himself and self-
> confident, and probably does not want anyone
> independent around him. And I with my inner insecurity
> and self-consciousness, that I have to do all the little jobs
> that I haven't done for 20 years. Of course it is my fault; I
> should have prepared my departure much better and
> much earlier; should have had at least a drawing for the
> most important apparatus, etc. Siegbahn said to me
> once, Debye wrote nothing about co-workers or
> assistants (I asked Debye to do that several times) and he
> has little room. To me that doesn't seem true, the
> institute looks empty, there are few people around. But
> the important thing is that I came with such empty
> hands. Now Siegbahn will gradually believe—especially
> after your beautiful results—that I never did anything
> and that you also did all the physics in Dahlem. I am
> gradually losing all my courage. Forgive this unhappy
> letter. I never wrote how bad it really is.

February 6, 1939 Stockholm, Sweden

Lise, slowly realizing that she was being written out of the fission
discovery, confided in her brother Walter:

> Hahn has just published[xxvii] absolutely wonderful things
> based on our work together—uranium and thorium
> nuclei split into lighter nuclei such as barium and

lanthanum, krypton, strontium, etc. And much as these results make me happy for Hahn, both personally and scientifically, many people here must think I contributed absolutely nothing to it—and now I am so discouraged; although I believe I used to do good work, now I have lost my self-confidence.

February 11, 1939 Stockholm, Sweden and Copenhagen, Denmark

Lise Meitner and Otto Robert Frisch publish their letter to the editor in Nature, "Disintegration of Uranium by Neutrons: A New Type of Nuclear Reaction." In it, Lise explains the theory behind Hahn and Strassmann's findings:

> It seems therefore possible[xxviii] that the uranium nucleus has only small stability of form, and may, after neutron capture, divide itself into two nuclei of roughly equal size (the precise ratio of sizes depending on finer structural features and perhaps partly on chance). These two nuclei will repel each other and should gain a total kinetic energy of c. 200 Mev., as calculated from nuclear radius and charge... The whole 'fission' process can thus be described in an essentially classical way.

For the first time, the concept of nuclear fission was introduced, both as a new term and a new physics.

March 1939 Copenhagen, Denmark

Physicists worldwide were quick to realize the enormous energetic potential in nuclear fission. Among the physicists writing about this potential were Frederic Joliot of Paris and Enrico Fermi of New York. They saw that each time a nucleus split into roughly equal halves, neutrons would be given off. Uranium seemingly had the makings of a chain reaction which was initiated by neutrons, and potentially sustained by the neutrons from its own nucleus.

Frisch recalls that his

immediate answer was that[xxix] in that case no uranium ore deposits could exist: they would have been blown up long ago by the explosive multiplication of neutrons in them! But I quickly saw that my argument was too naive; ores contained lots of other elements which might swallow up the neutrons; and the seams were perhaps thin, and then most of the neutrons would escape. With that, the exciting vision arose that by assembling enough pure uranium (with appropriate care!) one might start a controlled chain reaction and liberate nuclear energy on a scale that mattered. Of course, the spectre of the bomb was there as well.

Ores indeed swallowed up neutrons, but pure uranium rich in the fissile uranium isotope U-235 would work. To get uranium rich in U-235, it would have to be enriched. To do so, first the uranium ore would have to be mined, and then subjected to various chemical processes to extract the uranium from its ore, and concentrated as uranium oxide, known as "yellowcake."

Yellowcake contained roughly 60% uranium. This high concentration of uranium was 90% U-238, the non-fissile isotope, and less than 1% fissile U-235. The process of obtaining a higher concentration of U-235 was known as enriching uranium.

Lise was staying in Copenhagen at the time, and worked with her nephew Frisch on verifying the fission fragments, looking to see if the decay products that were formerly identified as transuranes, elements of higher atomic number than uranium, were really lighter elements produced by fission. They setup their apparatus as follows. They irradiated a thin layer of uranium hydroxide with neutrons and the decay products that were light enough would land on a surface of water a millimeter away. Heavier decay products would remain embedded in the uranium. They plotted the half-lives of the lighter decay products they collected on the water and compared them to those they had previously believed to be transuranes. They found that the new decay curves exactly matched the previous transuranes. In other words, the transuranes that they had previously "discovered" had actually been lighter fission fragments all along.

They published their results in *Nature* on March 6, 1939 "Products of the Fission of the Uranium Nucleus."

At the end of March, Lise returned to Stockholm. She had cherished her time at Bohr's institute and dreaded returning to Manne Siegbahn's institute that not only didn't value her contribution, but didn't seem to want her there at all. No equipment, no lab assistant, and almost no communication, she was left to fend for herself.

Her sister and brother-in-law, however, had arrived from Vienna with some of their belongings, for which she appealed again to Otto Hahn. When would she get her belongings?

Otto replied:

> Your books were inspected[xxx], and some were removed. I had already taken away some Thomas Mann, Werfel, Zweig, etc., but I couldn't clear everything out, that would have been too obvious. Therefore now, e.g., the Lily Braun, Gorki, the rest of the Thomas Mann, etc., were taken. A pity, but nothing can be done.... Everything has become unbelievably strict.... Only one or two settings of silver may be sent out! [Everything] was packed, then came the new order and all the utensils had to be unpacked because of the silver, etc. How things stand right now, I don't know.

Leo Szilard had continued to focus his energies on developing a nuclear chain reaction. Being Jewish, he fled Germany and first emigrated to England, where he helped found the Academic Assistance Council to relocate refugee scientists, and subsequently emigrated to the United States on January 2, 1938.

When Szilard learned of fission from Niels Bohr in January 1939, he became convinced that he could use uranium to initiate and maintain that elusive chain reaction, and he set out to do so.

He asked Fermi to join him in developing a nuclear chain reaction. Fermi refused. So Szilard went it alone. Szilard got permission to use a laboratory at Columbia University for three months and borrowed money to fund his experiment. He obtained a beryllium cylinder which would serve as the source of neutrons from Oxford, and he brought on Walter Zinn as his collaborator.

Szilard and Zinn used a radium-beryllium source to irradiate uranium with neutrons and… nothing. Zinn realized that the oscilloscope setup to detect the radiation was not plugged in. As soon as Zinn remedied the situation, the two of them discovered a significant increase in the number of neutrons being produced by the irradiation over the number of neutrons that bombarded the uranium in the first place.

Szilard would later recall: "We turned the switch[xxxi] and saw the flashes. We watched them for a little while and then we switched everything off and went home… That night, there was very little doubt in my mind that the world was headed for grief."

With these results, Szilard was able to convince Fermi to try his experiment on a larger scale, though they would need a substance to absorb the excess neutrons. When water was used, too many neutrons were absorbed, leaving hardly enough to initiate the desired chain reaction. They then switched to graphite, a form of carbon, and proposed using heavy water, a form of water containing an isotope of hydrogen known as deuterium (so named because it contains both one proton and one neutron, having a mass number of 2).

On March 15, Nazi Germany invaded Czechoslovakia, in violation of the Munich Agreement.

March 13, 1939

England and France commit to protect Poland from Nazi German advances.

April 1939 Germany

Germany establishes a *Uranverein* (in English, a Uranium Society), a scientific effort to develop nuclear weapons.
April 29, 1939 Washington D.C.

That same month, an article appearing in the Washington Post titled "Physicists here debate whether experiments will blow up 2 miles of the landscape," showed the quick progression from the announcement of the fission discovery to its extrapolated end as a weapon of mass destruction.

July 12, 1939 New York

Concerned about the calamitous results if Germany were first to create an atomic bomb, Leo Szilard, along with physicist Eugene Wigner, took a drive to the town of Southold, in Suffolk County, on the Northeastern coast of Long Island, New York, a stone's throw across the river from Connecticut. The drive from New York City took almost three hours.

They pulled up to a home on Old Cove Road on Nassau Point, and got out of the car. The woman who answered the door ushered them to the back porch where their host Albert Einstein greeted them. Szilard did most of the talking.

As a result of their discussion, Szilard dictated a letter in German to the Belgian Ambassador to the United States, which Wigner transcribed and Einstein signed.

August 2, 1939 New York

In an effort to get governmental backing behind their uranium research, Szilard again set out for Long Island, this time with Edward Teller driving. Szilard had made contact with someone who could get a letter to the President of the United States himself.

On this second visit, Einstein dictated a letter in German, which Szilard dictated in English to a young stenographer Janet Coatesworth, upon returning to Columbia University. She later recalled that, when hearing this letter, she "was sure[xxxii] she was working for a nut."

The letter which was sent to and signed by Einstein, and delivered to the President Roosevelt went as follows:

Albert Einstein
Old Grove Rd.
Nassau Point
Peconic, Long Island

August 2nd 1939

F.D. Roosevelt
President of the United States
White House
Washington, D.C.

Sir:

Some recent work by E. Fermi and L. Szilard, which has been communicated to me in manuscript, leads me to expect that the element uranium may be turned into a new and important source of energy in the immediate future. Certain aspects of the situation which has arisen seem to call for watchfulness and, if necessary, quick action on the part of the Administration. I believe therefore that it is my duty to bring to your attention the following facts and recommendations:

In the course of the last four months it has been made probable - through the work of Joliot in France as well as Fermi and Szilard in America - that it may become possible to set up a nuclear chain reaction in a large mass of uranium, by which vast amounts of power and large quantities of new radium-like elements would be generated. Now it appears almost certain that this could be achieved in the immediate future.

This new phenomenon would also lead to the construction of bombs, and it is conceivable - though much less certain - that extremely powerful bombs of a new type may thus be constructed. A single bomb of this type, carried by boat and exploded in a port, might very well destroy the whole port together with some of the surrounding territory. However, such bombs might very well prove to be too heavy for transportation by air.

The United States has only very poor ores of uranium in moderate quantities. There is some good ore in Canada and the former Czechoslovakia, while the most important source of uranium is in the Belgian Congo.

In view of the situation you may think it desirable to have more permanent contact maintained between the Administration and the group of physicists working on chain reactions in America. One possible way of achieving this might be for you to entrust with this task a person who has your confidence and who could perhaps serve in an inofficial capacity. His task might comprise the following:

a) to approach Government Departments, keep them informed of the further development, and put forward recommendations for Government action, giving particular attention to the problem of securing a supply of uranium ore for the United States;

b) to speed up the experimental work, which is at present being carried on within the limits of the budgets of University laboratories, by providing funds, if such funds be required, through his contacts with private persons who are willing to make contributions for this cause, and perhaps also by obtaining the cooperation of industrial laboratories which have the necessary equipment.

I understand that Germany has actually stopped the sale of uranium from the Czechoslovakian mines which she has taken over. That she should have taken such early action might perhaps be understood on the ground that the son of the German Under-Secretary of State, von Weizsäcker, is attached to the Kaiser-Wilhelm-Institut in Berlin where some of the American work on uranium is now being repeated.

Yours very truly,

Albert Einstein

Leo Szilard's friend, economist Alexander Sachs, brought the letter to Roosevelt. Roosevelt responded, "Alex, what you are after is to see that the Nazi's don't blow us up."

"Precisely," replied Sachs.

To an aide, Roosevelt directed, "This requires action."

August 24, 1939 Moscow, Russia

Hitler and Stalin surprised the world by signing a non-aggression pact, stating that neither party would take military action against each other for the next 10 years. As a result, Hitler would be able to invade Poland without opposition from Russia. For Stalin, the pact bought time to build up Russia's forces against Nazi Germany. They agreed to divide up Eastern Europe among themselves after the war.

September 1, 1939 Poland

Germany invaded Poland by air and by land, using its "blitzkrieg" strategy. Germany assaulted Poland by air first, destroying Poland's air capacity, its railroads, communication lines and its munitions dumps. Then it followed up with an overwhelming display of tanks, troops and artillery. Finally, it moved in its infantry.

That same day, the second *Uranverein* (Uranium Club) was established, under military control, to research the building of a nuclear weapon. The first *Uranverein* had been dissolved as its three original proponents had been drafted for military service.

September 3, 1939 Europe

England and France declare war on Germany.

September 16, 1939 Germany

The second *Uranverein* convenes for the first time. Members and contributors to the *Uranverein* included Otto Hahn and Werner Heisenberg.

October 21, 1939 United States

The United States' own Uranium club, as it were, called the Advisory Committee on Uranium, met for the first time. President Roosevelt appointed Lyman J. Briggs, director of the National Bureau of Standards, to be its head.

The purpose of this early committee was to report on the current research on uranium and advise the president on next steps. The committee recommended funding of research on isotope separation as well as Enrico Fermi and Leo Szilard's work on fission chain reactions at Columbia University.

Isotope separation was essential in that only the uranium isotope U-235 was fissionable, which was far less abundant than U-238. Three methods were in development to separate these two isotopes from each other.

The first was centrifugation, which used high speed circular motion to separate a gaseous mixture of the two isotopes. The lighter isotope, having less inertia, was less affected by the centrifuge and could be drawn off at the center and top of the centrifuge.

The second was gaseous diffusion across a porous membrane that would allow the smaller U-235 particles to go through, leaving behind the larger U-238 particles.

And the third was liquid thermal diffusion, which used convection currents to carry the lighter U-235 particles to the top.

April 9, 1940 Copenhagen, Denmark

Nazi Germany took Denmark without a fight. Niels Bohr, who was Jewish by virtue of his mother, was now in special danger, as his laboratory housed one of the world's only particle accelerators. In addition, he was well-known for taking in Jewish refugee scientists.

Lise Meitner was at Bohr's laboratory in Copenhagen that day, though Bohr was not.

George de Hevesy, a Hungarian Jewish chemist and future Nobel laureate, quickly resorted to destroying paperwork that tied Bohr to his role in assisting Jewish refugees.

Further, Bohr was in possession of the Nobel Prizes of Max von Laue and James Franck, along with von Laue's Max Planck medal. Though it was illegal to take gold out of Germany at the time, von Laue and Franck and sent their medals to Copenhagen, a crime potentially resulting in capital punishment.

Bohr directed de Hevesy to destroy these medals. De Hevesy had first thought to bury the medals, but, as they were engraved with the scientists' names, their owners would have been in particular danger had these medals been unearthed. Then de Hevesy decided to dissolve them in aqua regia. Aqua regia is a solution of one-part concentrated hydrochloric acid and three-parts nitric acid. It was so named as the "water of kings" because of its ability to dissolve gold. De Hevesy spent the entire first day of the occupation frantically dissolving gold, a painstakingly slow process because gold was so characteristically difficult to dissolve.

When the Nazis ransacked Bohr's institute[xxxiii], they scoured the building for loot or evidence of wrongdoing but left the beaker of orange aqua regia untouched. De Hevesy was forced to flee to Stockholm in 1943, but when he returned to his battered laboratory after V-E Day, he found the innocuous beaker undisturbed on a shelf.

De Hevesy later described that day:

> After the occupation[xxxiv] of Copenhagen, your medals were Bohr's first concern. He was not interested in your medals but in your person. I proposed that we bury the medals, but since your name was engraved on them this did not satisfy Bohr. Dissolving the medals was the only way to make them disappear. I spent the entire first day of occupation with this not very easy task [this because gold is exceedingly unreactive and difficult to dissolve]…. [Later] the Nazis occupied Bohr's institute and searched everything very carefully, especially the vault where your medals had been stored. If they had found your medals in their original state, you would probably have landed in prison and would surely have wished you had never received them.

After the war, de Hevesy precipitated out the gold medal, and the Nobel Foundation recast them and re-presented them to von Laue and Franck in 1952.

Otto Robert Frisch had been in Birmingham at the outbreak of World War II, and remained there. There, at the University of Birmingham in 1940, he and the physicist Rudolf Peierls produced the Frisch–Peierls memorandum, outlining the process of using explosives to detonate a small critical mass of uranium-235 and predicted the results of such a powerful explosion.

Because Denmark was taken without a fight, the Germans left Denmark to its own self-government for a time. Denmark, throughout the occupation, refused to establish laws that discriminated against its Jews, and was thereby able to protect much of its Jewish population.

June 22, 1941 Russia

Germany double-crossed Stalin and invaded the Soviet Union.

June 27, 1940 United States

Up until this point, American research on nuclear fission had been published publicly in peer reviewed journals, as was the custom in all scientific research. When the National Defense Research Committee (NDRC) was established to replace the Advisory Committee on Uranium, all publication of U.S. scientific articles that had potential military relevance was halted.

December 14, 1940 Berkeley, California

After a number of false identifications in the early part of the century by Meitner and Hahn, the Joliot-Curies and Fermi, the first transuranic element neptunium, number 93, was discovered by Edwin McMillan and Philip H. Abelson using the cyclotron at Berkeley in 1940. The next transurane, plutonium, number 94, was discovered by Glenn Seaborg on December 14, 1940, by bombarding uranium-238 with deuterium, the isotope hydrogen-2, which temporarily formed the neptunium isotope Np-238, which decayed via beta decay to Pu-238.

By May 1941, Seaborg had shown how plutonium-239 was 1.7 times more likely than uranium-235 to undergo fission. As uranium was rare, and contained such a minuscule amount of fissile uranium-235, developing a fission bomb using plutonium became a likely candidate.

$$^{238}_{92}U + ^{1}_{0}n \rightarrow ^{239}_{92}Np$$

$$^{238}_{93}Np \rightarrow ^{238}_{94}Pu + ^{0}_{-1}e$$

September 15-21, 1941 Copenhagen, Denmark

Werner Heisenberg traveled to Copenhagen to participate in a German-sponsored scientific conference, in which Bohr refused to participate. Bohr, however, did agree to meet with Heisenberg during his stay.

By this time, Heisenberg was confident in Germany's ultimate victory, as the German army had invaded Russia and almost completely cut off Leningrad from the rest of the Soviet Union.

Bohr, on the other hand, resentful of the Nazi-occupation of Denmark, did not and would not concede defeat.
The conversation turned to the use of nuclear fission to build nuclear weapons. They took their conversation outside, presumably on September 17, for fear that Bohr's laboratory was bugged.

There has been much speculation as to the content of their conversation, but Bohr recalled 16 years later, in an unsent letter, the following:

> Dear Heisenberg,
>
> I have seen a book, "*Stærkere end tusind sole*" ["Brighter than a thousand suns"] by Robert Jungk, recently published in Danish, and I think that I owe it to you to tell you that I am greatly amazed to see how much your memory has deceived you in your letter to the author of the book, excerpts of which are printed in the Danish edition.
>
> Personally, I remember every word of our conversations, which took place on a background of extreme sorrow and tension for us here in Denmark. In particular, it made a strong impression both on Margrethe and me, and on everyone at the Institute that the two of you spoke to, that you and Weizsäcker expressed your definite conviction that Germany would win and that it was therefore quite foolish for us to maintain the hope of a different outcome of the war and to be reticent as regards all German offers of cooperation. I also remember quite clearly our conversation in my room at

the Institute, where in vague terms you spoke in a manner that could only give me the firm impression that, under your leadership, everything was being done in Germany to develop atomic weapons and that you said that there was no need to talk about details since you were completely familiar with them and had spent the past two years working more or less exclusively on such preparations. I listened to this without speaking since [a] great matter for mankind was at issue in which, despite our personal friendship, we had to be regarded as representatives of two sides engaged in mortal combat.

That my silence and gravity, as you write in the letter, could be taken as an expression of shock at your reports that it was possible to make an atomic bomb is a quite peculiar misunderstanding, which must be due to the great tension in your own mind. From the day three years earlier when I realized that slow neutrons could only cause fission in Uranium 235 and not 238, it was of course obvious to me that a bomb with certain effect could be produced by separating the uraniums. In June 1939 I had even given a public lecture in Birmingham about uranium fission, where I talked about the effects of such a bomb but of course added that the technical preparations would be so large that one did not know how soon they could be overcome. If anything in my behaviour could be interpreted as shock, it did not derive from such reports but rather from the news, as I had to understand it, that Germany was participating vigorously in a race to be the first with atomic weapons.

Besides, at the time I knew nothing about how far one had already come in England and America, which I learned only the following year when I was able to go to England after being informed that the German occupation force in Denmark had made preparations for my arrest.

All this is of course just a rendition of what I remember clearly from our conversations, which subsequently were naturally the subject of thorough discussions at the Institute and with other trusted friends in Denmark. It is quite another matter that, at that time and ever since, I have always had the definite impression that you and Weizsäcker had arranged the symposium at the German Institute, in which I did not take part myself as a matter of principle, and the visit to us in order to assure yourselves that we suffered no harm and to try in every way to help us in our dangerous situation.

This letter is essentially just between the two of us, but because of the stir the book has already caused in Danish newspapers, I have thought it appropriate to relate the contents of the letter in confidence to the head of the Danish Foreign Office and to Ambassador Duckwitz.

October 9, 1941 Washington D.C.

Vannevar Bush, the head of the National Defense Research Committee met with President Franklin D. Roosevelt and Vice President Henry A. Wallace. He had brought with him a report from top British scientists as to the feasibility of building an atomic bomb within the next two years. Bush summarized the report and asked for the President's support to go ahead with the project. President Roosevelt authorized Bush and the Committee to research the construction needs, the costs and the timeline, and to return their findings to him.

November 6, 1941 Washington D.C.

The committee returned with its report that it would require a critical mass of between 2 and 100 kg of uranium-235 and that it could be enriched using centrifugal separation.

December 7, 1941 Hawaii, United States

At 7:48 am, Japanese fighter planes attacked the sleepy and unsuspecting U.S. military installation at Pearl Harbor, damaging or destroying eight U.S. Navy battleships. 2,403 Americans were killed and 1,178 others were wounded.

December 8, 1941 Washington D.C.

The United States declared war on Japan.

President Roosevelt gave the go-ahead to proceed with the development of an atomic bomb.

December 11, 1941 Berlin, Germany and Washington, D.C.

Hitler, in a speech to the Reichstag, unilaterally declared war on the United States.

The United States Congress declared war upon Germany hours later.

January 20, 1942 outside of Berlin, Germany

Reinhard Heydrich, chief of the Reich Security Main Office convened the Wannsee Conference in a villa outside Berlin, at which he presented the plans for the "Final Solution of the Jewish Question."

March 1, 1942 Poland

German authorities opened a second camp at Auschwitz, called Auschwitz-Birkenau.

March 17, 1942 Poland

The first deportation of Jews to killing centers was carried out. Jews were deported from the ghettos in Lublin and Lvov, to the Belzec killing center. At Belzec, the SS killed at least 434,508 Jews in gas chambers using carbon monoxide gas between March 17 and December 31, 1942.

March 22, 1942 Berlin, Germany

The mass deportation of Jews continued. Arnold Berliner, former editor of *Naturwissenschaften*, had been ordered to vacate his apartment and was to be deported the following day.

Max von Laue wrote to Lise regarding Berliner:

> About our ... 80-year-old[xxxv], here on Kielganstrasse, Kielganstrasse, things look bad for him. No one knows what will happen to him next week. He is tired of living, but then speaks in a very animated manner about everything possible as soon as he is distracted from his personal situation.

That same night, Berliner committed suicide by drinking poison.

Max von Laue, later hearing of the details of that night, wrote:

> Kielgan [code name for Berliner] ... spoke with his housekeeper[xxxvi] until 11:30 that night, distributed books, cleared up other things, which she thought was related to his move to another—not yet found—apartment. The only unusual thing was that he adamantly refused ... to have a warm evening meal. Kielgan then did not go to bed, and the next day, when his housekeeper came from her job in the long-distance telephone office, she found him, cold and stiff in his armchair, sitting up. ... I miss Kielgan very much. He was one of those rare people with whom one could talk about things other than the commonplace, and in whom one could confide completely. Since you left, he was really the last person with whom I could do that.... His last words, as I left him at noon on the 22d, were that I must not be sad. He surely would have said the same to you.

October 1942 Chicago, Illinois

A young 38-year-old theoretical physicist came to the University of Chicago named Robert Oppenheimer.

May 1943 United States

It seemed as if the United States was no closer to building a bomb than it was when Roosevelt first received Einstein's letter.

There were two proposed pathways, the fission of uranium-235 and the fission of plutonium. And, there were three methods of separating the isotopes, by gaseous diffusion, centrifuge, and electromagnetic/thermal. They had not reached a conclusion by this time as to which was the most efficacious direction.

It was almost guaranteed that the Germans who themselves had discovered fission, were further ahead in the development of the bomb than the Americans, who had just entered the world theater.

Beyond creating a self-sustaining fission reaction, constructing the bomb itself was another major consideration and project in itself.

For security reasons, the atomic bomb project was placed under the auspices of the Army Corp of Engineers.

August 13, 1943 United States

The Manhattan Engineer District was established, under the Army Corps of Engineers to construct a fissionable weapon.

September 17, 1943 United States

Colonel (soon to be Brigadier General) Leslie R. Groves was appointed to head what was now commonly referred to as the Manhattan Project. Though an army man, Groves was an engineer who helped direct the building of the Pentagon and was well-equipped to lead scientific and engineering projects.

Groves immediately secured a site in Oak Ridge, Tennessee to produce plutonium, and enrich uranium using two different methods, the electromagnetic separation process and the separation process by gaseous diffusion.

Groves selected J. Robert Oppenheimer to head the project's secret weapons laboratory, where the bomb would be engineered and constructed. Oppenheimer was an odd choice in that he didn't have a Nobel prize to his name, and even more so, that he had flirted with communism while in college; and yet, at the same time, a brilliant choice.

Nobel Prize-winning physicist Isador Rabi called the choice of Oppenheimer "a real stroke of genius[xxxvii] on the part of General Groves, who was not generally considered to be a genius."

They secured a site at a boys' boarding school in Los Alamos, New Mexico, to be the central location of the project.

September 28, 1943 Copenhagen, Denmark

German diplomat Georg Ferdinand Duckwitz secretly informed the Danish resistance that the order to arrest and deport the Danish Jews was imminent. The Danish resistance responded quickly.

Up until that point, despite numerous offers, Niels Bohr had refused to leave Denmark. "Why should I leave?" he was known to say. "*They* should leave!" But now he and his brother had a choice. Stay and be deported out of Denmark, or flee. It was hardly a choice.

September 29, 1943 Copenhagen, Denmark

Niels Bohr and his wife Margarethe walked down a Copenhagen street where they met one of Bohr's colleagues, a biochemistry professor, who gave the Bohrs a secret sign. From there, they proceeded to a popular recreational beach where they "ran into" his brother Harald and his family. The boat trip would take two hours to cross the narrow body of water separating Denmark and Sweden. The fishermen were keenly aware of the German patrol schedule, and planned their path accordingly. The Bohr's reached Swedish shore two hours later.

In total, 7200 Danish Jews were ferried by fishing boats to neighboring Sweden. The rest of Copenhagen's large Jewish population fled the city by automobile, train and by foot. Many Jews who remained were hidden by their neighbors.

September 30, 1943 Stockholm, Sweden

Niels Bohr took an express train to Stockholm to meet with Swedish officials, including the secretary of state and King Gustaf V of Sweden, whom he persuaded to make Sweden's willingness to accept Jewish refugees public.

Bohr was still not particularly safe in Sweden, as an arrest warrant was issued by the Nazi government. The British urged him to come to England, and sent a de Havilland Mosquito aircraft to pick him up. The Mosquitos were high-speed bomber aircraft whose bomb bays had been converted to carry cargo or passengers. Because of their high-speed and ability to fly at high altitudes, they could avoid German fighters. They would need this versatility as Norway, separating Sweden and England, was German-occupied. A second aircraft was sent a week later for Bohr's son Aage. Bohr's wife stayed in Sweden.

Bohr, outfitted with a parachute, flying suit and oxygen mask lied on a mattress in the Mosquito's bomb bay. Because his helmet was too small, Bohr didn't hear the pilot's instructions to don his oxygen mask, and passed out from lack of oxygen. He revived later when the plane descended to lower altitudes.

Bohr was welcomed in London by James Chadwick. Despite being in Allied England, Chadwick kept Bohr out of site for his protection.

November 1942 Los Alamos, New Mexico

The Los Alamos school and its grounds were purchased by the United States Army's Manhattan Engineer District.

Oppenheimer brought into the project the greatest scientific minds he could gather, including Niels Bohr, Edward Teller, Otto Robert Frisch, Hans Bethe and Richard Feynman.

Brigadier General Leslie Groves, concerned that the Germans not only were making their own atomic bomb, but were far ahead of the U.S., established the Alsos Mission, tasked with investigating the Axis scientific research.

December 8, 1943 Washington D.C.

Bohr arrived in Washington D.C. with his son Aage as his assistant, where he met Groves, the director of the Manhattan Project. He visited Einstein and Pauli at the Institute for Advanced Study in Princeton, New Jersey, and went from there to Los Alamos, New Mexico.

Lise had also been approached by the British contingent to join the Los Alamos group.

We know that she was asked a second time by her nephew Otto Robert Frisch.

Los Alamos would have given Lise the ability to work on cutting-edge physics, to be among physics colleagues and would have relieved her of the isolation she felt in Manne Siegbahn's lab in Stockholm. And yet, she refused both times saying, "I will have nothing to do with the bomb."

February 1944 Los Alamos, New Mexico

Scientists and other staff converged on Los Alamos tasked with doing something that never had been done before, using a science that had just recently been discovered — that of creating a fission bomb. They believed they had the science to do it, but they lacked the engineering to put it together. The job at Los Alamos was to design that engineering — the goal, to devise a system whereby a subcritical mass of fissionable material was made critical.

There were two methods under consideration. One such method was a gun method. Two subcritical masses of enriched uranium were shot together to form the critical mass necessary and begin the detonation. This method, however, worked only with uranium-235. Plutonium underwent spontaneous fission continually, producing neutrons at a sufficiently high rate that the two subcritical masses would predetonate before they ever were shot together.

For plutonium, the scientists and engineered worked on an implosion method. For implosion to work, they would need to develop the engineering to apply uniform compression to the plutonium sample.

With both uranium and plutonium, they needed to design a bomb that would release energy efficiently at the right time, and in a casing that an airplane could deliver.

Meanwhile, the science of preparing the materials for fission was assigned to the teams at Oak Ridge, Tennessee and the University of Chicago.

In Oak Ridge, Tennessee, they had built miles and miles of piping to deposit uranium metal from a uranium-enriched gas by means of gaseous diffusion, and further refined that uranium using a combination of thermal diffusion and electromagnetic separation.

Glenn Seaborg had assembled a team at the University of Chicago, including Enrico Fermi and Leo Szilard, to create the first sustainable and predictable chain reaction. Working under the bleachers of University of Chicago's Stagg Stadium, they were successful in creating a chain reaction in Chicago Pile Number One, or CP-1 for short, which consisted of 40,000 graphite blocks enclosing 19,000 pieces of embedded uranium metal and uranium oxide fuel.

June 21, 1944 Stockholm, Sweden

Lise wrote to her friend Eva Bahr-Bergius about her fear that the Germans would find a path to the atomic bomb. "I am disturbed[xxxviii] to think that it may be possible to make uranium bombs after all."

July 20, 1944 Rastenburg, Prussia

High German officials, realizing that Hitler was running them into a suicidal end to the war, plotted to assassinate Hitler and salvage what was left of the war effort.

Colonel Claus von Stauffenberg, chief of the army reserve, was given the task of planting the bomb, which he placed under the table at which Hitler would be seated. Hitler and Colonel Heinz Brandt were studying a map of the Eastern front when Brandt moved the briefcase out of the way to get a better view. The bomb went off at 12:42 pm. Four of those present were killed but Hitler, although injured, survived.

Stauffenberg and his co-conspirator General Olbricht were shot that day, and over the next few months, 7000 Germans were be arrested, 5000 of whom died from execution or suicide. One of those arrested was Erwin Planck, Max Planck's son.

October 25, 1944 Berlin, Germany

Max Planck pleaded for his son's life in a personal letter to Hitler:

Mein Führer![xxxix]

I am most deeply shaken by the message that my son Erwin has been sentenced to death by the People's Court.

The acknowledgment for my achievements in service of our fatherland, which you, my Führer, have expressed towards me in repeated and most honoring way, makes me confident that you will lend your ear to an imploring 87-year old.

As the gratitude of the German people for my life's work, which has become an everlasting intellectual wealth of Germany, I am pleading for my son's life.

Max Planck

January 23, 1945 Berlin, Germany

Despite Max Planck's pleading, Erwin Planck was hanged to death at the at Plötzensee Prison in Berlin.

January 26, 1935 Berlin, Germany

Poland had fallen to the Soviets. The Soviet forces were continuing toward Berlin from the east. The American forces were approaching from the south on their way to Mainz, Mannheim, and the Rhine. The German troops in Italy were retreating north.

With Allied victories mounting, Hitler retreated to his bunker.

April 1, 1945 Okinawa, Japan
With the war in the west all but over, at dawn, the Fifth Fleet bombarded Okinawa with artillery, cushioning the landing of troops on shore. Though they were not immediately met by opposing Japanese forces, the Japanese were lying in wait.

April 12, 1945 Warm Springs, Georgia

President Roosevelt died of a massive cerebral hemorrhage.

April 12, 1945 7:00 pm The White House Washington, D.C.

President Harry S. Truman was sworn in as the 33rd President of the United States in the Cabinet Room of the White House. In offering his condolences to Eleanor Roosevelt, he said to her, "Is there anything[xl] I can do for you?" To which Eleanor replied, "Is there anything we can do for *you*? For you are the one in trouble now."

April 23, 1945 Haigerloch, Hechingen and Tailfingen, Germany

French troops entered Haigerloch where members of the Alsos mission found an experimental nuclear reactor in the cellar of a laboratory, but its uranium and heavy water were missing. The scientists dismantled the reactor, and found a sealed drum of documents in a cesspool, as well as three drums of heavy water and 1.5 tons of uranium ingots buried in a field. The scientists dismantled the nuclear reactor and loaded the uranium and heavy water onto trucks.

Some of their contingent continued onto Hechingen, where Werner Heisenberg's lab was supposed to be located. Others proceeded to Tailfingen, where they took Otto Hahn and nine members of his staff into custody.

When they arrived in Hechengen, they found that Heisenberg had already left on April 19, but von Weizsäcker and Max von Laue, and 23 others, were taken into custody.

May 1, 1945 Urfeld, Germany

Lieutenant Colonel Pash, the Alsos mission's commander, with a unit of ten men in two armored cars and two jeeps pursued Heisenberg to Urfeld, where they encountered heavy artillery.

May 2, 1945 Urfeld, Germany

Pash found Heisenberg at his home and took him into custody.

April 24, 1945 Washington, D.C.

Twelve days after Truman was sworn in as the 33rd President, Secretary of War Harry Stimson and General Leslie Groves informed him of the Manhattan Project. Truman agreed to continue the work at Los Alamos, even though the war on the European front was nearly over, as a protective deterrent to Stalin's Communist advances into Eastern Europe.

April 30, 1945 Berlin, Germany

With Allied and Soviet forces converging on Berlin, Hitler shot himself to death in his bunker.

May 7, 1945 Reims, France

Germany surrendered to the Allies, officially ending the European war. German Alfred Jodl of the German High command signed the official surrender in Reims, France, which would go into effect the following day.

May 8, 1945 Europe

May 8 was declared VE Day, the day of Victory in Europe.

June 22, 1945 Okinawa, Japan

The Battle of Okinawa finally ended, with the ritual suicides of General Ushijima and his Chief of Staff, General Cho. The battle lasted almost three months, and exacted a dreadful toll on the American war machine, especially in loss of life. In all, 36 ships were sunk, 368 were damaged, 763 aircraft were lost, 4900 men were killed and 4800 wounded. Many Japanese soldiers chose suicide over being captured, and it was becoming increasing evident that, even if the Japanese had no chance of winning the war, they would fight to the bitter end. It seemed that, to the Japanese, surrender was not an option.

July 3, 1945 Godmanchester, England

Ten captured German nuclear scientists were brought to England and interned at Farm Hall, a house in Godmanchester, near Cambridge.

They were:

Erich Bagge
Kurt Diebner
Walther Gerlach
Otto Hahn
Paul Harteck
Werner Heisenberg
Horst Korsching
Max von Laue
Carl Friedrich von Weizsäcker
Karl Wirtz

They would remain there until January 3, 1946, long after the war ended. The rooms of Far Hall were bugged, the Allies wanting to know how far the Germans had advanced in making a nuclear bomb. Due to a combination of German Nazi disorganization and the expulsion of an overwhelming percentage of Germany's top physicists, it turned out that Germany was further from making a bomb than the Allies had believed. In Farm Hall, however, the physicists attributed their inability to create a bomb as some sort of moral superiority over those who did.

July 16, 1945 Alamogordo, New Mexico

Trinity.

Physicists, engineers and technicians setup tents on the plains of Alamogordo, though few slept the night before. The rain and lighting at midnight threatened to delay their plans. Some were up all night checking weather, waiting for a clearing.

General Groves would later recall that night: "At Alamogordo[xli], we had about three hours or four hours to wait for the bomb. The tents were flapping in the high wind. [James B.] Conant and [Vannevar] Bush were in the same tent with me. Afterwards they asked, 'How on earth did you sleep? You went right to sleep while we stayed awake. With those tents flapping, how could you sleep?'

At 2 am, the weather started looking better and by 4 am, the rain stopped altogether. The clouds were rolling away by 4:45 am and the team agreed that it would be a go at 5:30 am.

A few hours before dawn that same day, the primary components of the gun type of uranium bomb were being hoisted onto the cruiser USS Indianapolis, setting sail for Tinian, one of the Northern Mariana Islands.

At 5:09 and 45 seconds, the master switches were unlocked, and countdown began T-20 minutes. Physicist Marvin Wilkening[xlii] recalled, "There was a countdown by Sam Allison, the first time in my life I ever heard anyone count backwards."

Those present at the test site were given welder's glasses and told to cover their eyes and lie face down, with their feet toward the blast.

No one knew whether the bomb would work at all. Or, if it would work too well. Edward McMillan had prepared his wife:

"We know that there are three possibilities. One, that we will all be blown to bits, if it is more powerful than we expect. If this happens, you and the world will be immediately told. Two, it may be a complete dud. If this happens, you will also be told. Third, it may as we hope be a success. We pray without loss of any lives. In this case, there will be a broadcast to the world with a plausible explanation for the noise and the tremendous flash of light which will appear in the sky."

The test bomb went off at 5:29 am that morning.

Val Fitch recalled that moment: "First the flash of light, that enormous fireball, the mushroom cloud rising thousands of feet in the sky, and then, a long time afterwards, the sound. The rumble, thunder in the mountains. Words haven't been invented to describe it in any accurate way."

German refugee and physicist Hans Courant described his reaction: "My hands got warm[xliii] from the heat from the bomb, which just grew and grew, and then eventually started up into the sky. But, I had been sitting there and I thought, 'Oh, my God.'"

July 21, 1945 Washington, D.C.

Looking as if the war in Japan would never end, President Truman gave Harry Stimson the handwritten order to release the bomb when ready, but not sooner than August 2.

July 23, 1945 Washington D.C.

Secretary of War Stimson brought the following top-secret communication to Truman about the readiness of the bomb:

Operation may be possible[xliv] any time from August 1 depending on state of preparation of patient and condition of atmosphere. From point of view of patient only, some chance August 1 to 3, good chance August 4 to 5 and barring unexpected relapse almost certain before August 10.

July 24, 1945 Potsdam, Germany

At 11:30 am in the dining room of Number 2 Kaiserstrasse, Harry Truman and Winston Churchill sat down with the American and British Chiefs of Staff, advising them that they would, barring the unconditional surrender of Japan, drop the atomic bomb.

Later that same day, Truman informed Josef Stalin. Truman would later recall:

"I casually mentioned[xlv] to Stalin that we had a new weapon of unusual destructive force. All he said was that he was glad to hear it and hoped we would make 'good use of it against the Japanese.'"

Stalin did not inquire more about it. Truman believed he didn't understand the implications of their communication. But Stalin understood more than Truman realized, because of his spy at Los Alamos, Klaus Fuchs.

July 26, 1945 Potsdam, Germany

Nine weeks after the surrender of Germany, President Truman, along with the newly elected Prime Minister of the United Kingdom Clement Atlee and Chairman of China Chiang Kai-shek, issued the Potsdam Declaration, defining the terms for the surrender of Japan. If Japan failed to surrender, the declaration continued, it would face "prompt and utter destruction."

July 30, 1945 Pacific Ocean

The USS Indianapolis, which had carried the parts of the atomic bomb Little Boy to the Mariana Islands, was torpedoed and sunk by the Imperial Japanese Navy submarine I-58 in 12 minutes. Of its 1196 crewman, 300 went down with the ship, while the rest faced sun exposure, dehydration, sharks and salt water poisoning while awaiting rescue. They were spotted four days later. Of the 900 crewman that had survived the initial attack, only 317 survived.

August 2, 1945 Potsdam, Germany to Plymouth, England

Truman left Potsdam by motorcade. He went by plane to Plymouth, England, where he would board the SS Augusta, bound for the United States.

Before leaving, Truman had lunch aboard the British battleship HMS Reknown with King George VI. After lunch, King George VI accompanied Truman to the SS Augusta, where he inspected the guard, "took a snort of 'Haig & Haig,'" and requested three of Truman's autographs, one for the Queen, and one for each of his two daughters, Princess Elizabeth and Princess Margaret.

That day, the SS Augusta set sail for the United States.

August 3, 1945 Atlantic Ocean

Truman summoned the members of the press who had accompanied him on board, and informed them about the history leading up to the atomic bomb.

August 4, 1945 Atlantic Ocean

Truman spent the day reading reports and working on an address to the country.

August 5, 1945 Atlantic Ocean, Leksand, Dalecaria and the Mariana Islands

Truman attended Sunday morning church services, and resumed his work the rest of the day.

Lise Meitner had left Stockholm for a brief respite in Leksand, Dalecaria to enjoy the quiet of the countryside.

At 1500 hours in the Marianas, Gen. LeMay officially confirmed the mission for the next day.

Colonel Paul W. Tibbets, Jr. assumed command of the Boeing B-29 Superfortress bomber that would drop the atomic bomb. He named it Enola Gay, after his mother, Enola Gay Tibbets, and had its name painted on the craft.

Later, he would recall that "my thoughts turned[xlvi] at this point to my courageous red-haired mother, whose quiet confidence had been a source of strength to me since boyhood, and particularly during the soul-searching period when I decided to give up a medical career to become a military pilot. At a time when Dad had thought I had lost my marbles, she had taken my side and said, 'I know you will be all right, son.'"

August 6, 1945 The Mariana Islands to Hiroshima, Japan

0000 hours[xlvii].

At zero hundred hours, Colonel Tibbets briefed the crews of all seven planes involved in the day's mission. Chaplain William Downey delivered a prayer he composed for the occasion. At 0112 hours, trucks picked up the crews for the two observation planes that would accompany the Enola Gay, The Great Artiste and Necessary Evil. At 0115 hours, a truck picked up Tibbets and the rest of the crew of the Enola Gay.

At 0137 hours, the three weather planes, Straight Flush, Jabit III, and Full House took off, each designated to separately assess the weather conditions over Hiroshima, Kokura, and Nagasaki. At 0151 hours, Big Stink takes off as standby over Iwo Jima.

At 0220 hours, Enola Gay was lit up with flood lights, cameras were flashing, and bystanders waved. Colonel Tibbets had to yell out of the cockpit for the bystanders to get out of the way because they were about to roll. To oblige the onlookers, Tibbets leaned out of the cockpit of the Enola Gay and waved to the cameras. Tibbets turned to his crew and says, "Okay, let's go to work," and started its engines. The Enola Gay taxied to its position on the runway.

At 0245 hours, Colonel Paul Tibbets and his co-pilot Robert Lewis taxied down the runway, picked up speed and then pushed all throttles forward. The overloaded Enola Gay lifted slowly into the night sky, needing all of the more than two miles of runway.

Within minutes, the two accompanying planes, The Great Artiste and Necessary Evil took off.

At 0300 hours, Capt. William "Deak" Parsons and Morris Jeppson prepared Little Boy by inserting the gunpowder and the detonator, and then climbed out of the bomb bay.

At 0600 hours, the B-29s met over Iwo Jima, climbed to 9,300 feet, and set course for Japan.

At 0715 hours, Jeppson removed Little Boy's safety devices and inserted the arming devices. Tibbets announced to the crew, "We are carrying the world's first atomic bomb." Inwardly, he was reminded of the first time he had killed civilians in combat. He had commanded a team of 100 bombers to attack industrial targets in the French city of Lille, on October 9, 1942, which unwittingly resulted in many civilian casualties. At the time, he tried to reason away the death of innocents. He reminded himself that his medical school colleagues who didn't make it were the ones who were too sympathetic to their patients to perform their duties to the best of their abilities. Tibbets had a job to do and a target to hit. And it was his job to do it to the best of his abilities. Still, he carried that day with him.

The Enola Gay began its ascent to 32,700 feet.

Aboard the USS Augusta, Truman spent the morning on deck listening to the ship's band.

0809 hours: The weather planes fly over their possible target cities.

0824 hours: The pilot of the Straight Flush weather plane sent Tibbets a coded message that stated: "Cloud cover less than 3/10ths at all altitudes. Advice: bomb primary." Tibbets announced to the crew, "It's Hiroshima." Richard Nelson sent a one-word message to William L. Uanna, squadron security chief on Iwo Jima: "Primary."

At 0831 hours, the weather planes departed their locations. In Hiroshima, the all-clear was sounded.

At 0905 hours, the city of Hiroshima first came into view. At 0914 hours, Tibbets told his crew, "On glasses."

At 0914:17 (0814:17 Hiroshima time), the 60-second sequence to automatically release the bomb was engaged.

At 0915:15 (8:15:15 Hiroshima time): The bomb bay doors opened, and Little Boy was dropped from the plane. Ferebee announced, "Bomb away." Tibbets immediately turned the Enola Gay to the right.

By the time the bomb exploded, Enola Gay had already flown eleven and a half miles away. Tibbets recalled "observing a silver blue flash and experiencing a strange feeling in his mouth, the same feeling as if he touched the lead and silver fillings in his mouth with a fork."

Aboard the SS Augusta, Truman ate lunch with some of the crew in the after mess. Just before noon, a Map Room officer handed him a communication from the Secretary of War that Hiroshima had been bombed four hours earlier. "Results clear-cut[xlviii] successful in all respects. Visible effects greater than in any test."

The decision to drop the atomic bomb would forever vilify Truman in the eyes of many. It's reasonably certain, however, that Roosevelt would have done the same had he lived. And, with the casualties of war still being inflicted on the American side in a war that was for one, unwinnable by the Japanese and secondly, for all intents and purposes over, to still have to send American troops home in body bags was too great a toll.

Truman would remark later:

> I asked General Marshall what it would cost in lives to land on the Tokyo plain and other places in Japan. It was his opinion that such an invasion would cost at a minimum a quarter of a million American casualties... It occurred to me that a quarter of a million of the flower of our young manhood were worth a couple of Japanese cities, and I still think they were and are.

70,000–80,000 people were killed by the blast and its firestorm that day, of which 70% were civilians.

August 7, 1945 Leksand, Dalecaria

Lise first learned of the atomic bomb when a reporter called the next morning. The news was so jarring that she felt it necessary to escape outside for a five hour walk. When she returned, she was met by reporters, photographers and a stack of telephone messages.

She permitted to be interviewed by the *Stockholm Expressen* which published the interview under the heading: "Fleeing Jewess," describing her as the woman who fled from Germany, taking the bomb secrets with her and giving them to the Allies.

August 9, 1945 Nagasaki, Japan

Japan having not surrendered after the bombing of Hiroshima, the second atomic bomb, the plutonium implosion bomb, nicknamed Fat Boy, was released over Nagasaki at 11:02 am.

At least 35,000–40,000 people were killed in Nagasaki and 60,000 others injured.

That night, Lise was interviewed on a radio program by Eleanor Roosevelt, remotely from a radio station in Leksand. She recalled the painful experience:

> Nothing was tested[xlix]. I did not know how loud I should speak, or how close to the microphone to be. Mrs. R. began. I understood only half of it and lost my composure when I answered. Much too near the microphone, and too soft. It was quite idiotic. ... I was inwardly ashamed of my helplessness.

Unwittingly, the woman who would have "nothing to do with the bomb," was now the celebrity face of the bomb, replete with the moniker, "Jewish mother of the bomb."

August 15, 1945 Japan

Emperor Hirohito of Japan broadcast his surrender and acceptance of the Potsdam Declaration. The war was over.

November 15, 1945 Stockholm, Sweden

The Nobel committee announced that Otto Hahn, now an unwilling resident at Farm Hall, was the 1944 recipient of the Nobel Prize in Chemistry for "for his discovery of the fission of heavy nuclei." Lise Meitner never received a Nobel Prize for her earlier work, nor for her role in the discovery of nuclear fission.

November 20, 1945 Stockholm, Sweden

Lise was happy with Hahn's achievement. Still, she felt she deserved similar recognition, as she confided in a letter to her friend B. Broomé-Aminoff:

> Surely Hahn fully deserved the Nobel Prize in chemistry. There is really no doubt about it. But I believe that Otto Robert Frisch and I contributed something not insignificant to the clarification of the process of uranium fission – how it originates and that it produces so much energy, and that was something very remote from Hahn.

Still being held at Farm Hall, Hahn was unable to attend the prize ceremony. He would accept the prize in person the following year.

January 3, 1946 Godmanchester, England

The scientists at Farm Hall were released.

January 25, 1946 New York, New York

Lise arrived in New York on her first trip to the United States.

When she stepped from the plane she was met by a swarm of reporters and photographers. She was also met by both her sisters, who had emigrated to the U.S., and Otto Robert Frisch, who had traveled by train for two days and nights from Los Alamos.

February 9, 1936 New York, New York

Lise was named Woman of the Year by the Woman's National Press Club. At the banquet in her honor, she was seated next to President Truman, where he is reported to have said, "So you're the little lady who got us into all of this!"

Author's Note

I first heard of Lise Meitner in a PBS dramatization of the book $E=mc^2$. As a science major and science teacher, I would have thought I knew a great deal more about science than the general population. Learning about Lise Meitner for the first time, I realized how crucial it was to pass on these stories to the present and subsequent generations. It seems unfathomable that there are twentieth century scientists who have contributed so much to our basic knowledge of science and have been written out of the narrative because of their gender or their religion.

Since learning about Lise Meitner, I have created the website Rocket Girls to encourage girls and young women in the sciences, and I'm thrilled to continue bringing the stories of these "Rocket Girls" to light.

As I was writing this book, I realized how much of Lise's story has relevance for us today. Though women have far more choices in education and career than they had one hundred years ago, the genders are still not equally represented in the sciences. Even though women represent roughly half of all college students, and earn 50% of the undergraduate degrees in biology, women are not ascending the ranks at the rates of their male counterparts. There are fewer women earning masters degrees, and far fewer women earning Ph.Ds. And, if that weren't enough, a smaller percentage of women who do receive these higher degrees are actually employed in their representative fields than their male counterparts. The gender discrepancy in physics is especially pronounced.

But more than that, Lise's story is about science and truth in an age of nationalism, bigotry and censure. It's about opening doors to refugees, even when there is no more room for refugees. And it's about doing what is right, even when the price is too dear.

Lise's nephew Otto Robert Frisch inscribed on her headstone:

"A physicist who never lost her humanity."

I hope that, by writing this book, I in some small way bring the story of Lise Meitner to a new generation.

Here is a list of some of the people documented in this book.

Henri Becquerel (1852 - 1908)

French physicist who discovered radioactivity and along with the Curies, received the 1903 Nobel Prize in Physics.

Arnold Berliner (1862 - 1942)

German Jewish editor of the scientific journal *Naturwissenschaften*, Germany's version of the journal Nature.

Niels Bohr (1885 - 1962)

Danish physicist who developed the orbital model of the atom in which the electrons revolve around the nucleus in quantized orbits, and who received the 1922 Nobel Prize in Physics.

Ludwig Boltzmann (1844 - 1906)

Austrian physicist who developed statistical mechanics, which explains properties of atoms predict the physical properties of matter.

Carl Bosch (1874 - 1940)

German chemist who developed along with Fritz Haber the Bosch-Haber process of nitrogen fixation, and received the 1931 Nobel Prize in Chemistry.

Vannevar Bush (1890 - 1974)

American engineer and scientific administrator who was one of the early administrators of the Manhattan Project.

James Chadwick (1891 - 1974)

English physicist who discovered the neutron and for which, he received the 1935 Nobel Prize in Physics.

Dirk Coster (1889 - 1950)

Dutch physicist who, along with Georg de Hevesy, discovered the element Hafnium.

Marie Curie (1867 - 1934)

Polish physicist and chemist who discovered polonium and radium, and earned two Nobel Prizes, the 1903 Nobel Prize in Physics and the 1911 Nobel Prize in Chemistry.

Pierre Curie (1859 - 1906)

French physicist and husband of Marie Curie, who, along with his wife, received the 1903 Nobel Prize in Physics for their radiation research.

George de Hevesy (1885 - 1966)

Hungarian Jewish radiochemist who discovered Hafnium along with Dirk Coster, and received the 1943 Nobel Prize in Chemistry.

Peter Debye (1884 - 1966)

Dutch physicist who received the 1936 Nobel Prize in Chemistry for his "contributions to the study of molecular structure," primarily his work on dipole moments and X-ray diffraction.

Albert Einstein (1879 - 1955)

German Jewish physicist who discovered the theory of special relativity, $E=mc2$, the photoelectric effect and who received the 1921 Nobel Prize in Physics.

Elsa Einstein (1876 - 1936)

Second wife and first cousin of Albert Einstein.

Enrico Fermi (1901 - 1954)

Italian physicist, creator of the first nuclear chain reaction who received the 1938 Nobel Prize in Physics.

Adriaan Fokker (1887 - 1972)

Dutch physicist and inventor of the Fokker organ.

Otto Robert Frisch (1904 - 1979)

Austrian Jewish physicist and nephew of Lise Meitner, who along with Meitner, theorized the fission of uranium by Meitner and Hahn.

Leslie R. Groves (1896 - 1970)

United States Army Corps of Engineers officer who oversaw the construction of the Pentagon and directed the Manhattan Project.

Fritz Haber (1868 - 1934)

German Jewish chemist who developed the Haber process by which nitrogen from the atmosphere could be fixated in a form absorbable by plants. He is considered the Father of Chemical Warfare and received the 1918 Nobel Prize in Chemistry.

Otto Hahn (1879 - 1968)

German physicist who, along with Lise Meitner, discovered nuclear fission and the element protactinium, and who received the 1944 Nobel Prize in Chemistry.

Werner Heisenberg (1901 - 1976)

German physicist, founder of the Heisenberg Uncertainty Principle, key pioneer of quantum mechanics and received the 1932 Nobel Prize in Physics.

Frederic Joliot (1900 - 1958)

French physicist and husband of Irene Joliot-Curie who, along with his wife Irene, discovered artificial radioactivity and received the 1935 Nobel Prize in Chemistry.

Irene Joliot-Curie (1897 - 1956)

French physicist and daughter of Marie and Pierre Curie who discovered artificial radioactivity along with her husband Frederic, and received 1935 Nobel Prize in Chemistry.

Lise Meitner (1878 - 1968)

Austrian Jewish physicist who, along with Otto Hahn, discovered nuclear fission and the element protactinium.

J. Robert Oppenheimer (1904 - 1967)

American physicist and head of the Los Alamos Laboratory under the Manhattan Project.

Max Planck (1858 - 1947)

German physicist who originated quantum theory and received the 1918 Nobel Prize in Physics.

Wilhelm Roentgen (1835 - 1923)

German physicist who discovered X-rays and received the 1901 Nobel Prize in Physics.

Franklin D. Roosevelt (1882 - 1945)

32nd President of the United States who authorized the Manhattan Project.

Paul Rosbaud (1896 - 1963)

German metallurgist and scientific publisher who spied for England during World War II.

Ernest Rutherford (1871 - 1937)

British physicist born in New Zealand who discovered the nuclear decay products alpha and beta particles, discovered the nucleus of the atom, and received 1908 Nobel Prize in Chemistry.

Erwin Schrodinger (1887 - 1961)

Austrian physicist who developed the wave equation to predict the location and probability of electrons and received the 1933 Nobel Prize in Physics.

Manne Siegbahn (1886 - 1978)

Swedish physicist who was the Director of the Physics Department of the Nobel Institute of the Royal Swedish Academy of Sciences, and who received the 1924 Nobel Prize in Physics "for his discoveries and research in the field of X-ray spectroscopy."

Harry Stimson (1867 - 1950)

American politician who served as Secretary of War under Taft, FDR and Truman, and Secretary of State under Hoover.

Fritz Strassmann (1902 - 1980)

German chemist who worked alongside Otto Hahn and Lise Meitner, and helped identify the products of nuclear fission.

Leo Szilard (1898 - 1964)

Hungarian Jewish physicist who created the first nuclear chain reaction.

Paul W. Tibbets, Jr. (1915 - 2007)

US Air Force officer whose plane dropped the atomic bomb over Hiroshima.

Harry S. Truman (1884 - 1972)

33rd President of the United States who authorized the bombing of Hiroshima and Nagasaki.

Max von Laue (1879 - 1960)

German physicist who received the 1914 Nobel Prize in Physics for his discovery of the diffraction of X-rays by crystals.

Carl Friedrich von Weizsäcker (1912 - 2007)

German physicist who worked under Werner Heisenberg to develop the German atomic bomb.

---

[i] Sime, Ruth Lewin. Lise Meitner: A Life in Physics (California Studies in the History of Science) (p. 72). University of California Press. Kindle Edition.

[ii] Sime, Ruth Lewin. Lise Meitner: A Life in Physics (California Studies in the History of Science) (pp. 109-110). University of California Press. Kindle Edition.

[iii] Sime, Ruth Lewin. Lise Meitner: A Life in Physics (California Studies in the History of Science) (p. 142). University of California Press. Kindle Edition.

[iv] Hager, T. (2008). The alchemy of air: A Jewish genius, a doomed tycoon, and the scientific discovery that fed the world but fueled the rise of Hitler.

[v] Hager, T. (2008). The alchemy of air: A Jewish genius, a doomed tycoon, and the scientific discovery that fed the world but fueled the rise of Hitler.

[vi] Leo Szilard Papers. MSS 32. Special Collections & Archives, UC San Diego Library.

[vii] D. Hahn, Otto Hahn.

[viii] Spencer R. Weart and Gertrude Szilard, eds., Leo Szilard: His Version of the Facts (Cambridge: MIT Press, 1978), 13–14.

Sime, Ruth Lewin. Lise Meitner: A Life in Physics (California Studies in the History of Science) (p. 430). University of California Press. Kindle Edition.

[ix] Nature 136, 506-506; 28 September 1935

[x] "I will never forget the expression of intense joy …" Dry, Sarah. Curie. London: Haus Publishing, 2003; p. 124, as quoted in Conkling, Winifred. Radioactive!: How Irène Curie and Lise Meitner Revolutionized Science and Changed the World (Kindle Locations 2697-2699). Algonquin Books. Kindle Edition.

[xi] Irène Curie and F. Joliot,*Nature*,**133**, 201-202 ;1934..

[xii] Sime, Ruth Lewin. Lise Meitner: A Life in Physics. Berkeley, California: University of California Press, 1996; p. 162.

[xiii] Otto Frisch, What Little I Remember (Cambridge: Cambridge University Press, 1979), 88, as quoted in Sime, Ruth Lewin. Lise Meitner: A Life in Physics (California Studies in the History of Science) (p. 435). University of California Press. Kindle Edition.

[xiv] Sime, Ruth Lewin. Lise Meitner: A Life in Physics (California Studies in the History of Science) (p. 192). University of California Press. Kindle Edition.

[xv] Sime, Ruth Lewin. Lise Meitner: A Life in Physics (California Studies in the History of Science) (p. 212). University of California Press. Kindle Edition.

[xvi] Sime, Ruth Lewin. Lise Meitner: A Life in Physics (California Studies in the History of Science) (p. 217). University of California Press. Kindle Edition.

[xvii] Translated in Sime, Ruth Lewin. Lise Meitner: A Life in Physics (California Studies in the History of Science) (p. 451). University of California Press. Kindle Edition.*Kernspaltung*

[xviii] Conkling, Winifred. Radioactive!: How Irène Curie and Lise Meitner Revolutionized Science and Changed the World (Kindle Locations 1691-1693). Algonquin Books. Kindle Edition.

[xix] Conkling, Winifred. Radioactive!: How Irène Curie and Lise Meitner Revolutionized Science and Changed the World (Kindle Locations 1706-1708). Algonquin Books. Kindle Edition.

[xx] Conkling, Winifred. Radioactive!: How Irène Curie and Lise Meitner Revolutionized Science and Changed the World (Kindle Locations 1713-1715). Algonquin Books. Kindle Edition.

[xxi] Sime, Ruth Lewin. Lise Meitner: A Life in Physics (California Studies in the History of Science) (p. 236). University of California Press. Kindle Edition.

[xxii] Sime, Ruth Lewin. Lise Meitner: A Life in Physics (California Studies in the History of Science) (p. 243). University of California Press. Kindle Edition.

[xxiii] February 7 letter to Lise Meitner

[xxiv] Sime, Ruth Lewin. Lise Meitner: A Life in Physics (California Studies in the History of Science) (p. 249). University of California Press. Kindle Edition.

[xxv] https://www.atomicheritage.org/article/manhattan-project-spotlight-enrico-fermi

[xxvi] Sime, Ruth Lewin. Lise Meitner: A Life in Physics (California Studies in the History of Science) (pp. 254-255). University of California Press. Kindle Edition.

[xxvii] Sime, Ruth Lewin. Lise Meitner: A Life in Physics (California Studies in the History of Science) (p. 255). University of California Press. Kindle Edition.

[xxviii] *Nature*143,239–240(11 February 1939) doi:10.1038/143239a0

[xxix] Sime, Ruth Lewin. Lise Meitner: A Life in Physics (California Studies in the History of Science) (p. 261). University of California Press. Kindle Edition.

[xxx] Sime, Ruth Lewin. Lise Meitner: A Life in Physics (California Studies in the History of Science) (pp. 268-269). University of California Press. Kindle Edition.

[xxxi] Rhodes, Richard (1986). The Making of the Atomic Bomb. New York: Simon and Schuster, p. 291.

[xxxii] Lanouette, William; Silard, Bela (1992). Genius in the Shadows: A Biography of Leo Szilárd: The Man Behind The Bomb. New York: Charles Scribner's Sons, p. 202.

[xxxiii] Kean, Sam. (2011)*The disappearing spoon :and other true tales of madness, love, and the history of the world from the periodic table of the elements* New York : Back Bay Books,

[xxxiv] Sime, Ruth Lewin. Lise Meitner: A Life in Physics (California Studies in the History of Science) (p. 283). University of California Press. Kindle Edition.

[xxxv] Sime, Ruth Lewin. Lise Meitner: A Life in Physics (California Studies in the History of Science) (p. 297). University of California Press. Kindle Edition.

[xxxvi] Sime, Ruth Lewin. Lise Meitner: A Life in Physics (California Studies in the History of Science) (p. 297). University of California Press. Kindle Edition.

[xxxvii] Bird, Kai; Sherwin, Martin J. (2005). American Prometheus: The Triumph and Tragedy of J. Robert Oppenheimer. New York: Alfred A. Knopf, pp. 185–187.

[xxxviii] Sime, Ruth Lewin. Lise Meitner: A Life in Physics (California Studies in the History of Science) (p. 307). University of California

Press. Kindle Edition.

xxxix http://grahamfarmelo.com/max-planck-letter-hitler-discovered/ accessed 11/12/2017.

xl "Eleanor and Harry: The Correspondence of Eleanor Roosevelt and Harry S. Truman". Truman Library.

xli https://www.atomicheritage.org/article/remembering-trinity-test-0, accessed 11/17/2017

xlii https://www.atomicheritage.org/article/remembering-trinity-test-0, accessed 11/17/2017

xliii https://www.atomicheritage.org/article/remembering-trinity-test-0, accessed 11/17/2017

xliv McCullough, David. "Truman." Truman, Simon & Schuster, 1992, p. 437.

xlv McCullough, David. "Truman." Truman, Simon & Schuster, 1992, p. 442.

xlvi Tibbets, Paul W. (1998). Return of the Enola Gay. New Hope, Pennsylvania: Enola Gay Remembered Inc.

xlvii https://www.atomicheritage.org/history/hiroshima-and-nagasaki-bombing-timeline, accessed 11/18/2017.

xlviii McCullough, David. "Truman." Truman, Simon & Schuster, 1992, p. 454.

xlix Sime, Ruth Lewin. Lise Meitner: A Life in Physics (California Studies in the History of Science) (p. 314). University of California Press. Kindle Edition.

Made in the USA
Coppell, TX
21 November 2023

24521281R20080